CLAREESE HILL
LAWRENCE CHIAM
JONATHAN THOMAS
MAX SCHNEIDER
ELIN JONES
MARION LANCIAUX
GIAN GUIDO ZURLI
FERNANDA MONTORO
RAUL DIAZ
MARTIN CARTWRIGHT
EUGEN NOUJAEV
FRANTICHAM
EVER DUNDAS
EVAN CERDA
MELANIE J. ALEXANDROU
BEN INNOCENT
ROXANNE DANER
ALAN MARCHESELLI
ANDREW KUA
CÉCILE DE VRIES
BEN INNOCENT
BERND F. OEHMEN
BRITTA HERSHMAN
ENRICO FIENI
CANDICE MORATO
ELIZA AGOSTA
ERIK SOSSO
FERDINAND VYKOUKAL
GABRIELE PAGANI
GENEVIEVE NEAL
IGNAS KUTAVICIUS
INA ECHTERNACH
JAMES MATTHEW CARROLL
JOSEAN MOLINA
JONATHAN CAMPOLO

CHIHARU HOSHIDA
IGNAS KUTAVICIUS
KATIE SYKES
LENA BURGGRAEF
FRANK BROUWER
FEDERICO CORPIERI
MARIADONATA VILLA
MARIANNA BATTOCCHIO
DOROTA WAGNER
MASSIMILIANO MUNER
MASSIMO BATTISTA
MICHELA SCAGNETTI
MIRIAM VAN HOVEN
NUNO TUDELA
RUDY FORCE
GIOVANNA CHEMI
SEBASTIAN GULAK
TAYLOR SHURTE
TUNG CHU
TOM GALLAGHER
SUSANNA GAUNT
DOREEN STAHR
TOBIAS AND ANNE
ASCHENBRENNER
THOMAS HOFMANN
CHRISTIAN DYLONG
SARAH CROOKSTON
IGNAS KUTAVICIUS
MIK BOITIER
CLAUDIA MENG
DEBORAH YUN
BERND F. OEHMEN
CARMEN PALERMO
ANDREAS SCHIMANSKI
HANNAH DOUCET

EMILIE LEFELLIC
REMO CAMEROTA
DWAYNE LUTCHNA
IKEM NZERIBE
PAOLO MORI
KATIE SYKES
ALAN MARCHESELLI
CARMEN PALERMO
DANIEL GONZÁLEZ FUSTER
CARSTEN WOYWOOD
ALFREDO PRADO
WOLLE VAN DER LOHN
JOOST VERBURG &
KAREN GLANDRUP
BARBARA WERTH
KIMBERLEE OBERSKI
REMO CAMEROTA
CLAUDIA & FRIENDS
AVE HEIDELBERGER
WERONIKA GAJDA
ALAN MARCHESELLI
JOSIE KEEFE
GUILLAUME POLLINO
DANIEL DÖRING
BARBARA WERTH
ULRIKE KOBLER
LIA SÁILE
AVE HEIDELBERGER
IMPOSSIBLE FACTORY TEAM
JIMMY LAM
RAUL DIAZ
ROSANNA BARSON
FLORIAN KAPS

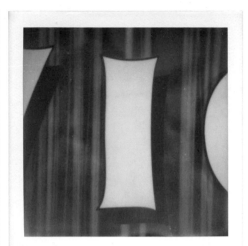

101 WAYS TO DO SOMETHING IMPOSSIBLE

AN ANALOG INSTANT PHOTOGRAPHY CHALLENGE

REINVENTING PHOTOGRAPHY

IMPOSSIBLE

WE ARE IMPOSSIBLE

Analog instant photography ranks among the greatest loves of our lives. Willing to do anything for this love, we took up the challenge to see it through after Polaroid ceased film production in 2008. First, we put all our efforts into preserving Polaroid's original production machinery, which was essential for the grand plan we had in mind: to invent and develop new instant films for classic Polaroid cameras. It was impossible to simply adopt the Polaroid film formula, due to several components that were missing or unavailable, so we had to start from scratch in our quest to carry analog instant film production into the 21st century.

The task of developing a completely new instant film seemed truly impossible in several ways, and even the most optimistic integral film experts doubted our venture would ever arrive at a happy ending. Perhaps that attitude was unsurprising, given the more than 30 new components like chemicals and layers we had to source and combine in a way that would lead to an instant photo. What never failed to inspire our hard-working team, and even led to our project's name, is a beautiful quote by Dr. Edwin H. Land, the founder and inventor of Polaroid: "Don't undertake a project unless it is manifestly important and nearly impossible."

HOW IMPOSSIBLE ARE YOU?

Having turned this important sentence into a mantra that kept us never giving up despite unexpected challenges and problems, we finally achieved our goal. Since 2010, we have been proud to present new instant films, made with love and dedicated to authenticity, originality, creativity, unpredictability and to the millions of Polaroid cameras and creative minds out there. Let your senses be touched, your creativity challenged, your ideas turned into reality. It's our sincere hope that you will fall in love with analog instant photography just as much as we have, and we invite you to come along with us the Impossible way.

Dr. Florian Kaps,
Founder of The Impossible Project

EXPERIENCE THE IMPOSSIBLE WORLD

When you hear the sound of the mechanical Polaroid shutter, when you wait patiently for your photo to develop, when you turn it over for the first time and when you hold that small universe in your hands, you just know – this is real! Unlike the many virtual tasks we pursue every day, analog instant photos belong truly and undeniably to the physical world surrounding us. You can feel their slight weight when you hold them in your hands and you can smell their fresh chemical scent. Touching your skin and wafting up to your nose, analog instant photography is not some intangible nostalgic state of mind, but something that exists in the real world.

In this irresistible and charming way, Impossible photos become one of the many elements in our lives, an element that despite its fixed physical shape – that legendary white frame – sets us at liberty to define the amount and quality of its significance.

Starting with the first newly invented Impossible instant film in 2010, users around the world have been essential in defining the role that analog instant photography will play in our digital 21st century. With constantly evolving projects and exhibitions taking place, it's become clear that this is more than a trendy vintage dalliance. Real and intelligent human beings everywhere are using Impossible instant film as a basis for their work, a medium that allows them to express and create highly individual ideas, feelings, opinions, projects, aims and styles. The ambition and spirit that underlie all these actions turn an Impossible photo from merely a tangible object into something that enriches, inspires, alienates, reflects, delights, interferes or changes the various spheres of our lives.

Once it had dawned on us what sheer endless potential could be found in the projects and results created by analog instant film photographers worldwide, we knew we wanted to get to the bottom of this phenomenon. In the winter of 2011–12, we put out a call for ideas of things you can do only and especially with Impossible photos. Collecting 101 projects seemed ambitious and slightly unrealistic at that point, so imagine our surprise and amazement when we soon received 315 projects. With so many diverse ideas on what to do with and how to approach Impossible photos, selecting only 101 for this book proved a challenging task.

With the selection in this book, we aim to show a wide range of ideas for what you can do with an Impossible photo once it's ejected from your Polaroid camera. From classics like image manipulation or double exposure to innovative ideas for gourmets and fashionistas,

from private to public, from the practical to the spiritual, the projects presented here are meant to inspire you and set your own creativity on fire. Detailed instructions on how to get going yourself can be found at the end of the book, as well as on our website.

There isn't just one way of doing it. Our Impossible Project Spaces around the world are also good starting points for plunging into your analog instant adventure. Discover and learn everything Impossible, meet new Impossible friends and celebrate Impossible artists – join us in New York, Paris, Vienna or Tokyo.

THE IMPOSSIBLE WORLD

UNIQUE IDEAS TRAVELED MILLIONS
OF MILES TO COME TOGETHER FOR
THIS COLLECTION.

WE COLLECTED 101 PROJECTS FROM
OVER 20 COUNTRIES AROUND THE
GLOBE.

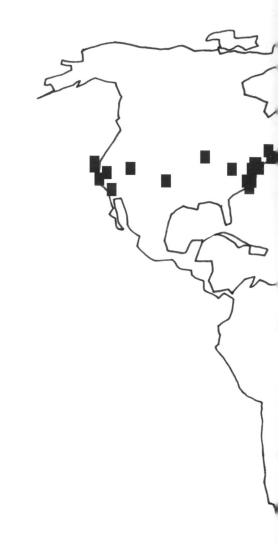

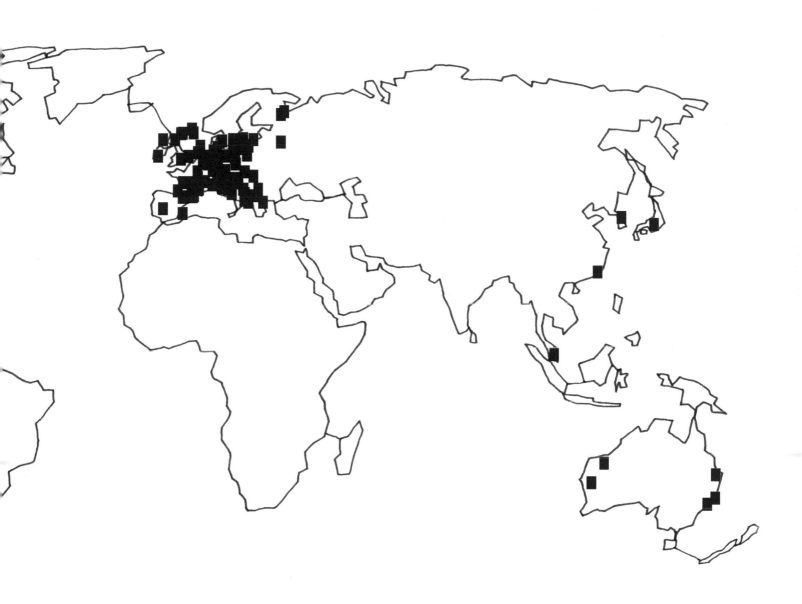

The magic of analog instant photography is unfolding around the whole globe. Creative and passionate people from all over the world have contributed their ideas on what to do with Impossible photos.

CATALOG

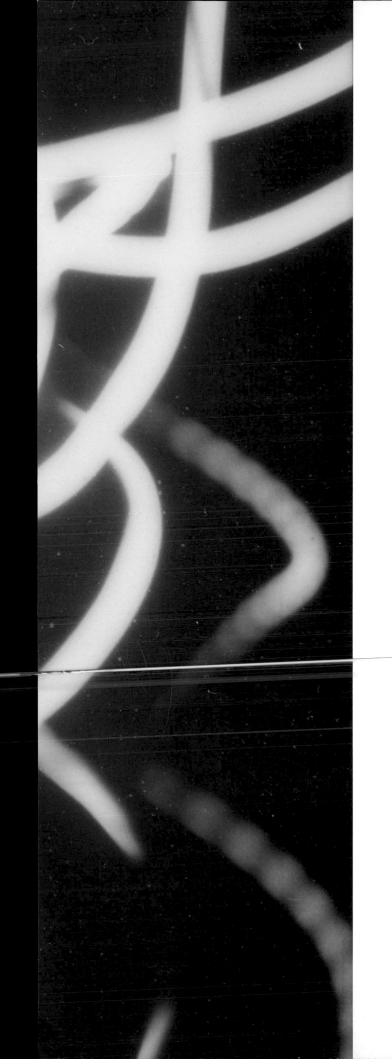

Clareese D Hill

**CLAREESE HILL
USA**

**PX 600 SILVER
SHADE**

**CAMERA:
SLR 680**

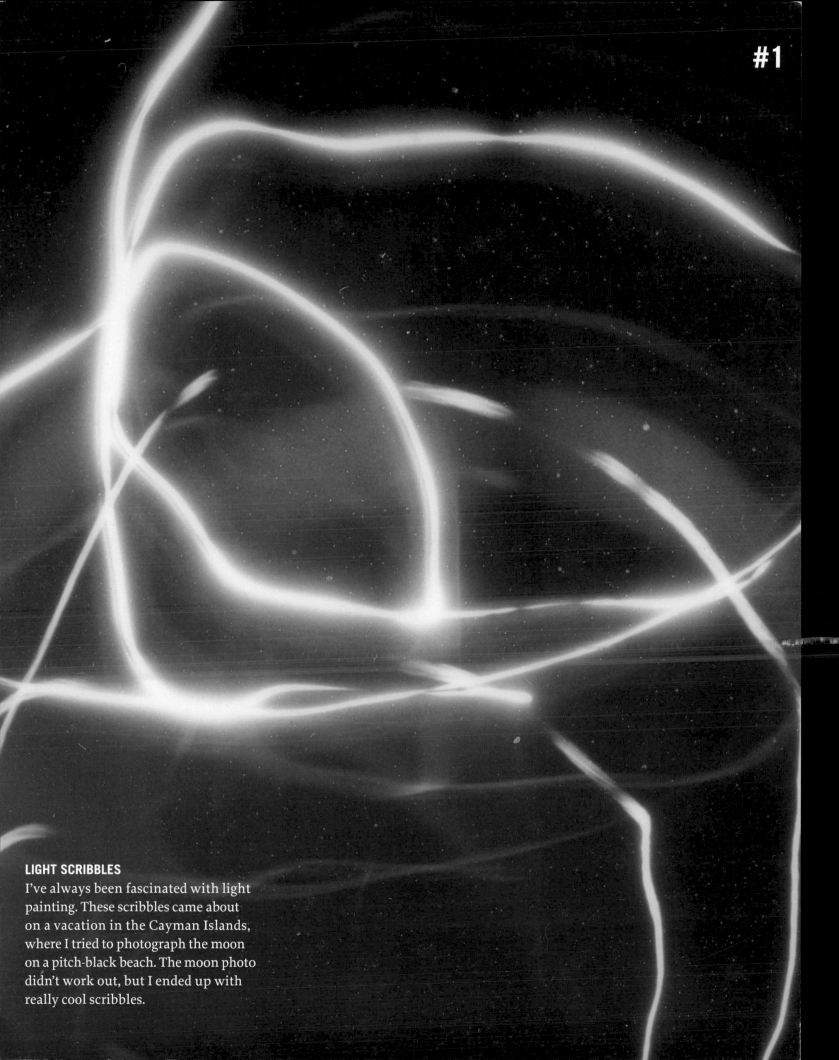

LIGHT SCRIBBLES

I've always been fascinated with light painting. These scribbles came about on a vacation in the Cayman Islands, where I tried to photograph the moon on a pitch-black beach. The moon photo didn't work out, but I ended up with really cool scribbles.

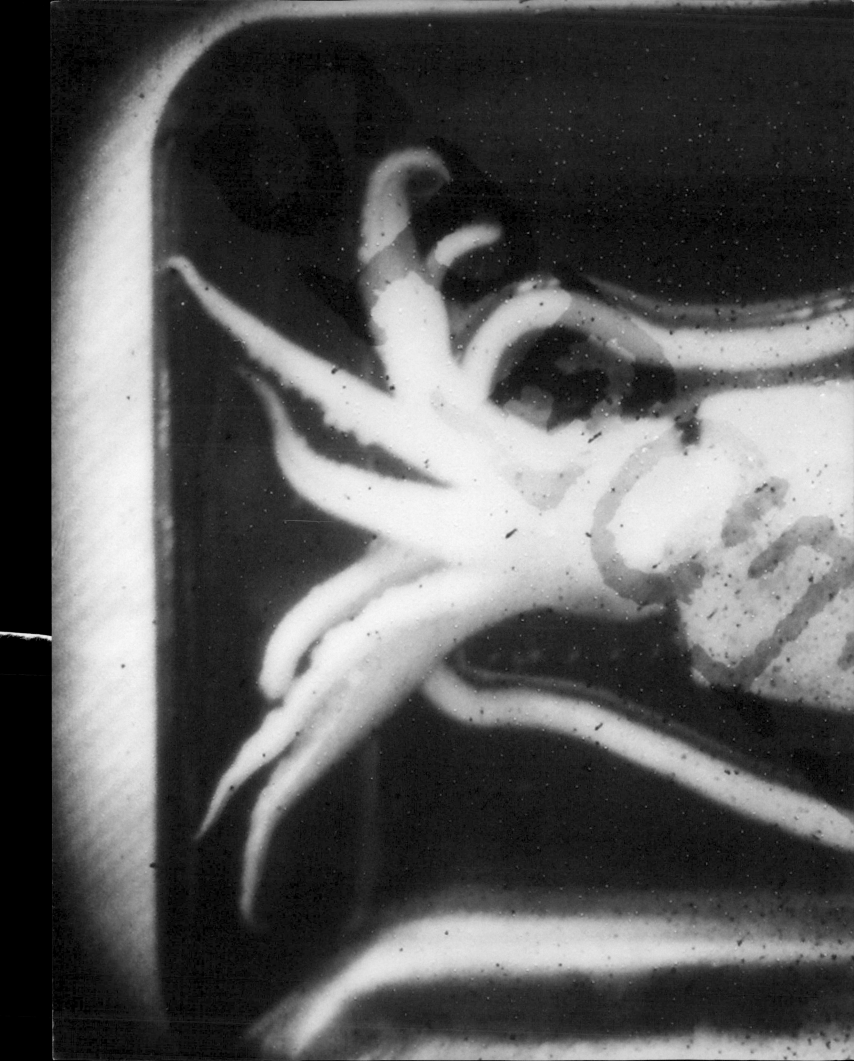

Lawrence Chiam ☺

LAWRENCE CHIAM
SINGAPORE

PZ600 SILVER
SHADE UV+ BLACK
FRAME

CAMERA:
IMAGE/SPECTRA
WITH POLAROID
CLOSE-UP-LENS

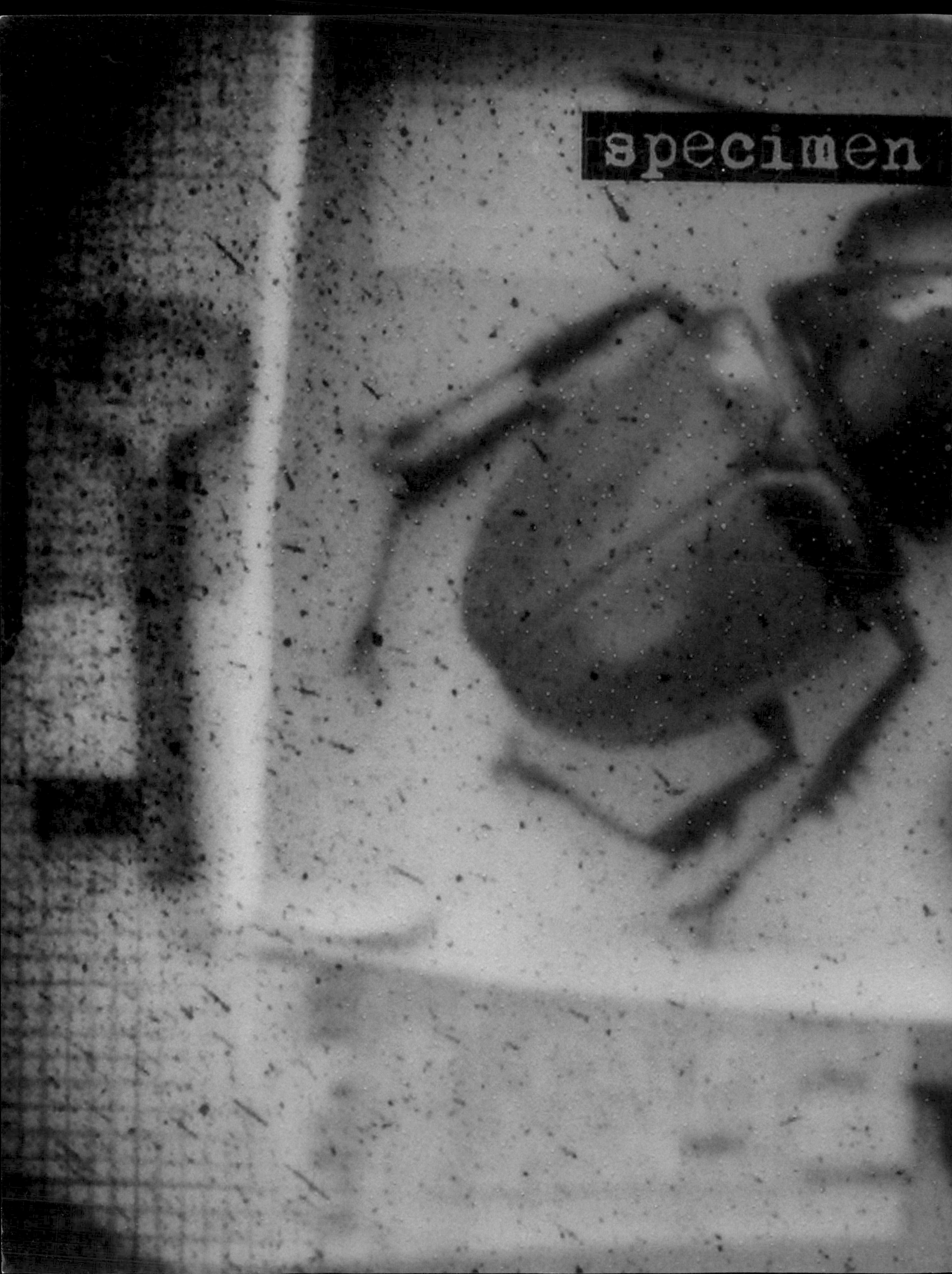
specimen

DESIGN YOUR OWN FILTER
Specimens: A Botanist's Strange En-
counters*. The Spectra camera's wide-
format film is ideal for the curious
scientist looking to document specimens
of the strange yet beautiful world of
living organisms.
*Part of the Thirtysix "Impossible
Lessons" Project.

**JONATHAN THOMAS
USA**

**PZ 680 COLOR
SHADE**

**CAMERA:
IMAGE / SPECTRA**

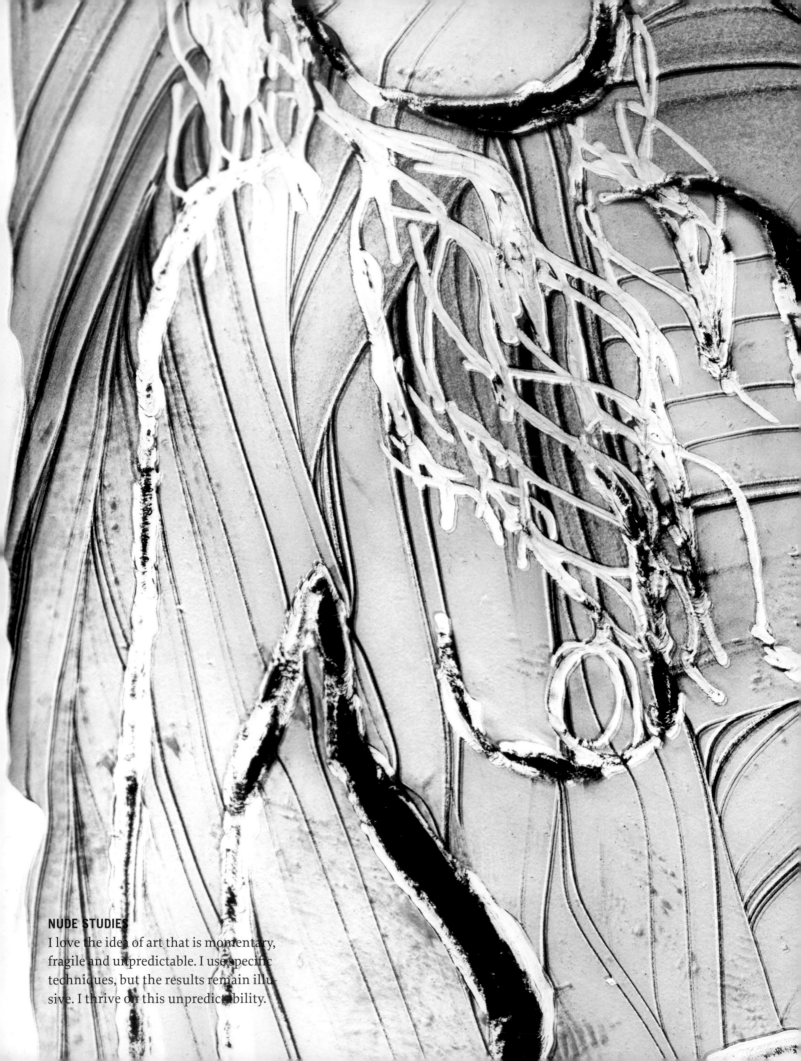

NUDE STUDIES
I love the idea of art that is momentary, fragile and unpredictable. I use specific techniques, but the results remain illusive. I thrive on this unpredictability.

#3

MAX SCHNEIDER

**MAX SCHNEIDER
GERMANY**

**PX 70 COLOR
SHADE**

**CAMERA:
SX 70**

POLAROID PAINTINGS
The analog instant chemistry defines the unique feel and quality of this medium. My photos pay tribute to the chemical process itself. Colors fade, blend, separate ... creating forms and patterns that resemble abstract paintings.

LIN JONES
VALES

X 600 SILVER
HADE UV+ BLACK
RAME

AMERA:
X 70 WITH
D FILTER

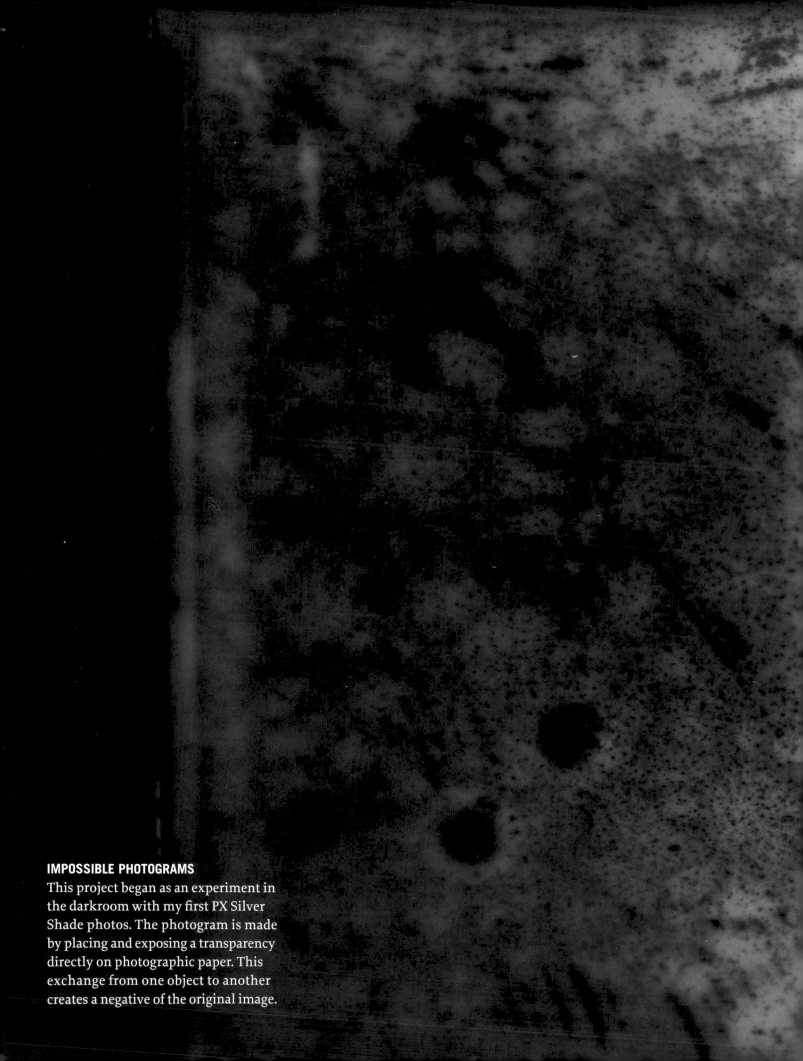

IMPOSSIBLE PHOTOGRAMS
This project began as an experiment in
the darkroom with my first PX Silver
Shade photos. The photogram is made
by placing and exposing a transparency
directly on photographic paper. This
exchange from one object to another
creates a negative of the original image.

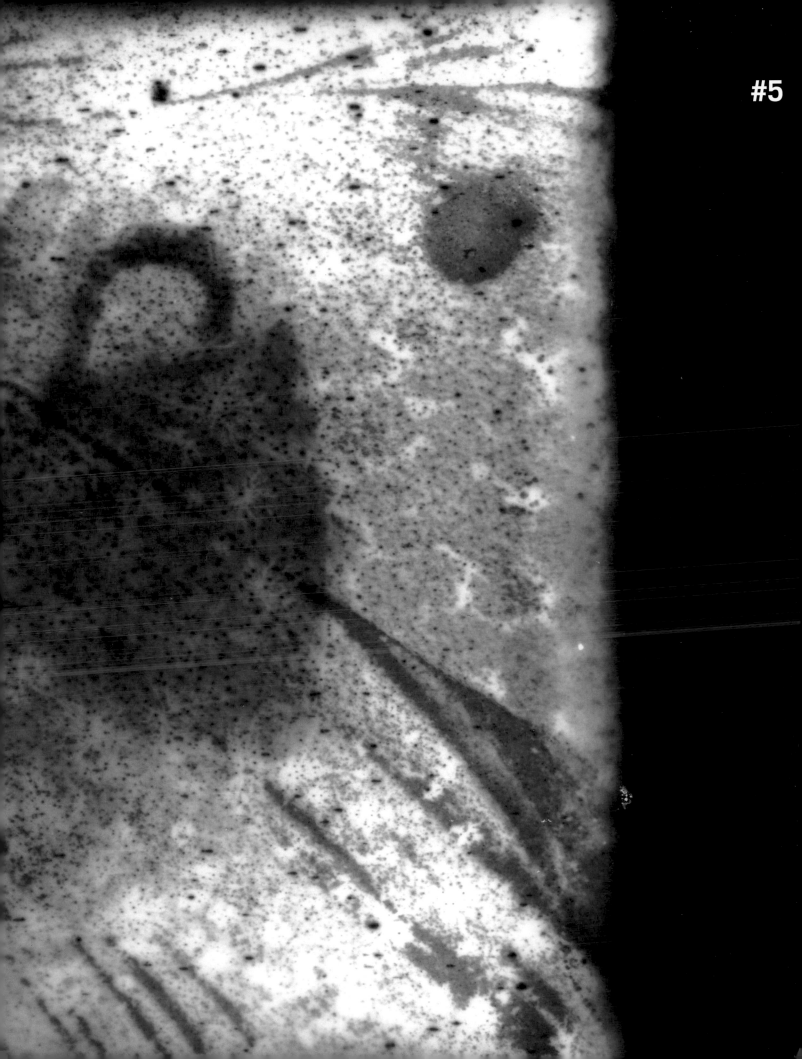

#5

ll hold spiritual joys and afterwards

ow can the real body ever die and b

Marion Lanciaux

**MARION LANCIAUX
FRANCE**

**PX 70 COLOR
SHADE**

**CAMERA:
SX 70 SONAR**

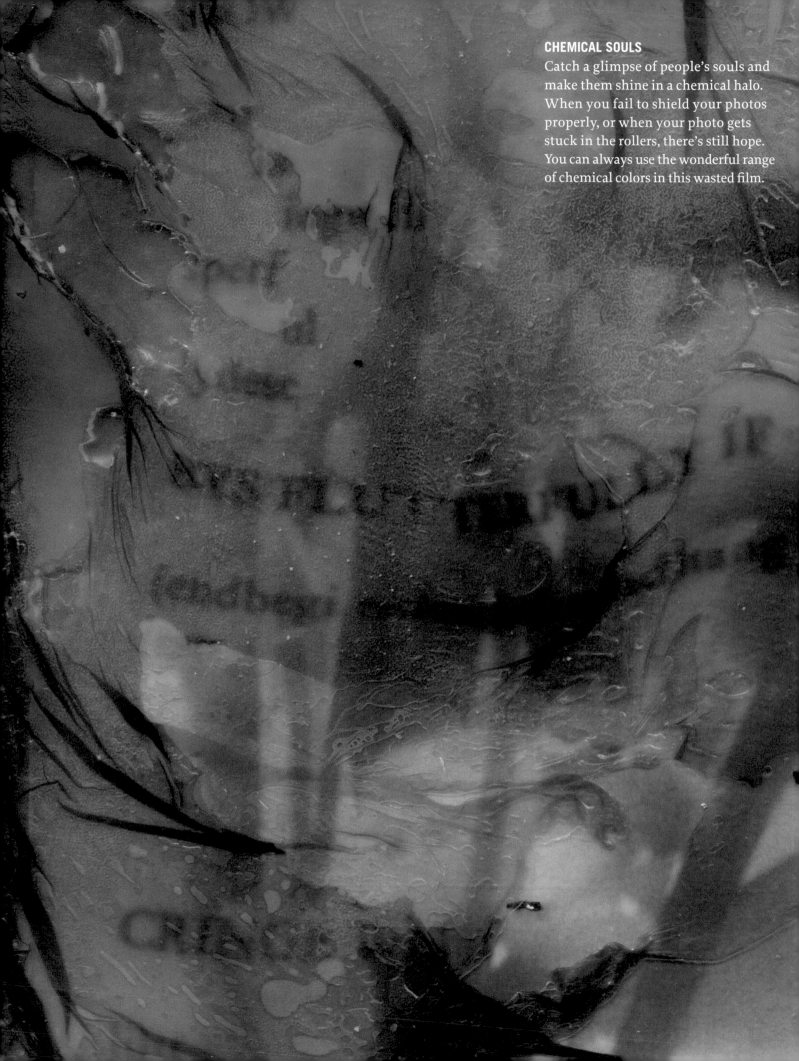

CHEMICAL SOULS
Catch a glimpse of people's souls and make them shine in a chemical halo. When you fail to shield your photos properly, or when your photo gets stuck in the rollers, there's still hope. You can always use the wonderful range of chemical colors in this wasted film.

FIRENZE

F

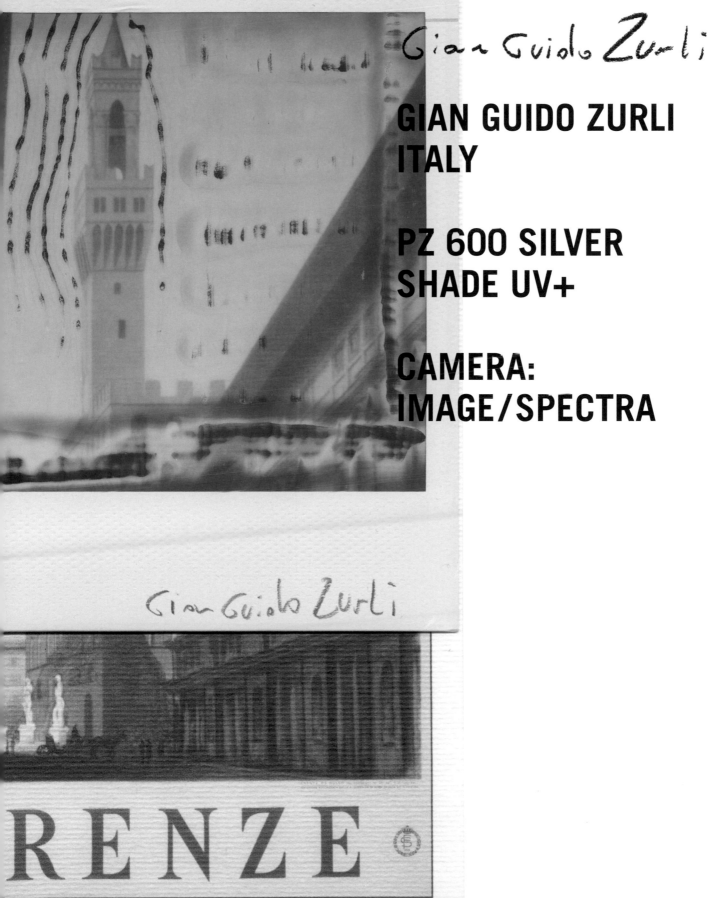

GIAN GUIDO ZURLI
ITALY

PZ 600 SILVER
SHADE UV+

CAMERA:
IMAGE/SPECTRA

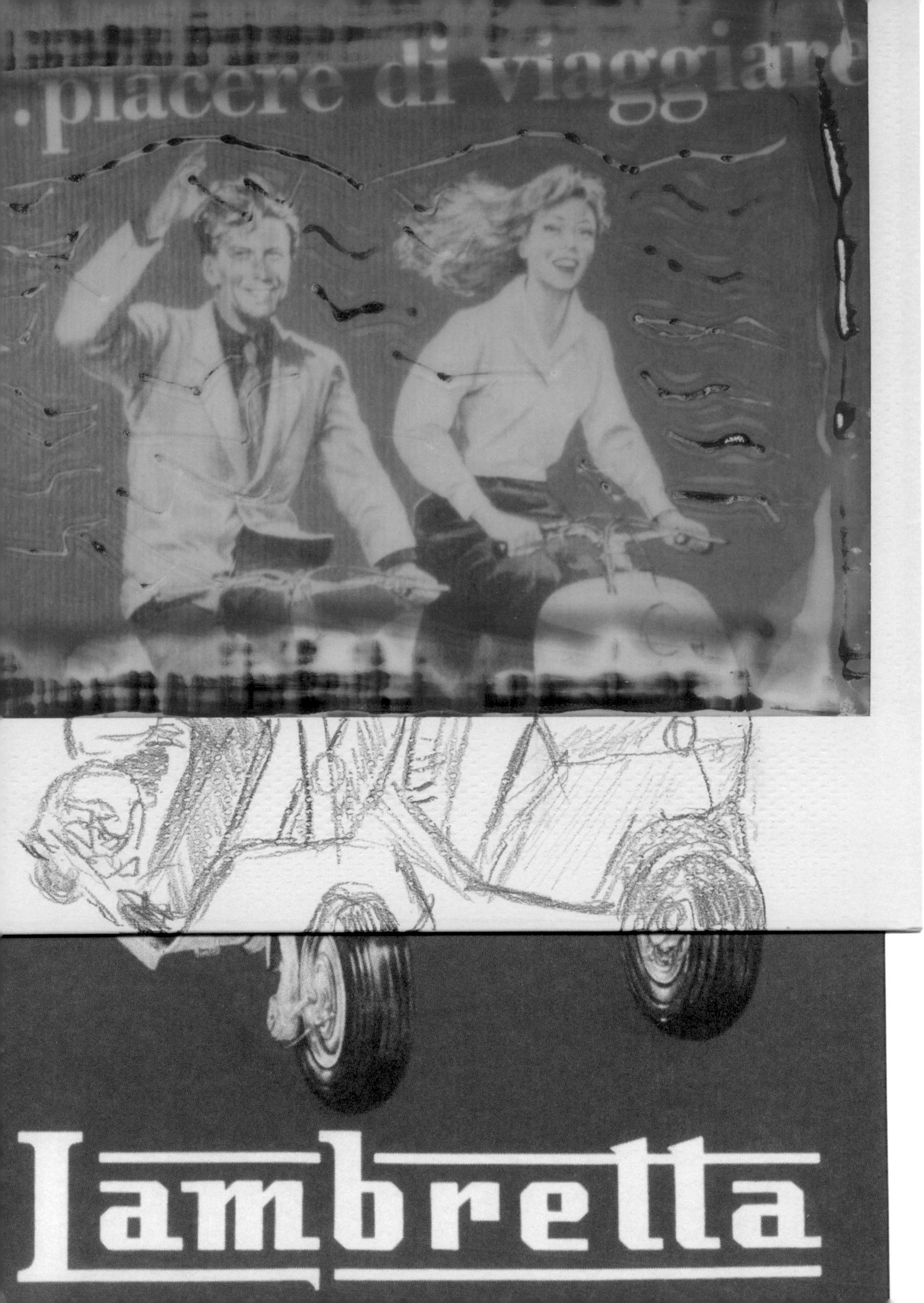
piacere di viaggiare
Lambretta

READY-MADE

Ready-mades, invented by Marcel Duchamp, are everyday manufactured goods deemed to be art merely by virtue of the artist selecting them as such. Maurizio Galimberti introduced ready-mades with original Polaroid films. Here the story continues with Impossible films.

fernanda Montoro

**FERNANDA MONTORO
URUGUAY**

**PX 70 COLOR
SHADE**

**CAMERA:
SX 70**

HEAVENLY CREATURES
Transform anyone into an enlightened,
heavenly creature – even your most
boring friend or enemy can become one
with this light painting technique!

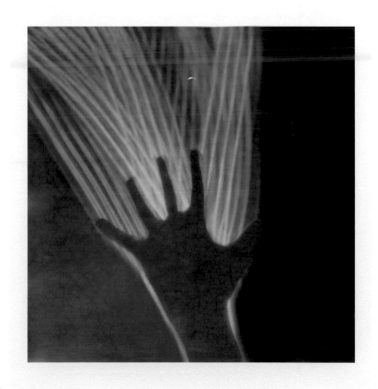

RAUL DIAZ
FRANCE

PX 100 SILVER
SHADE

PX 680 COLOR
SHADE

CAMERAS:
ALPHA 1 MODEL 2
SLR 680

SUPER WIDE
I've always been inspired by the big screen. By using multiple shots, I have managed to create one panoramic picture, emulating a cinematic feel with instant photos.

#9

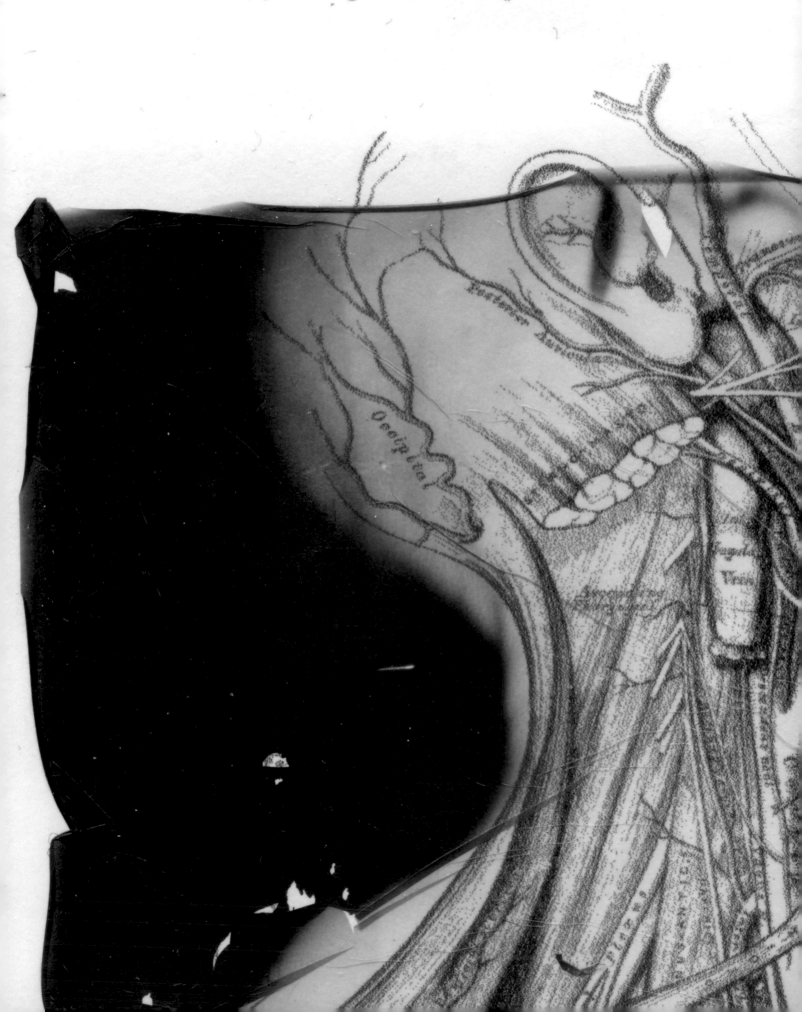

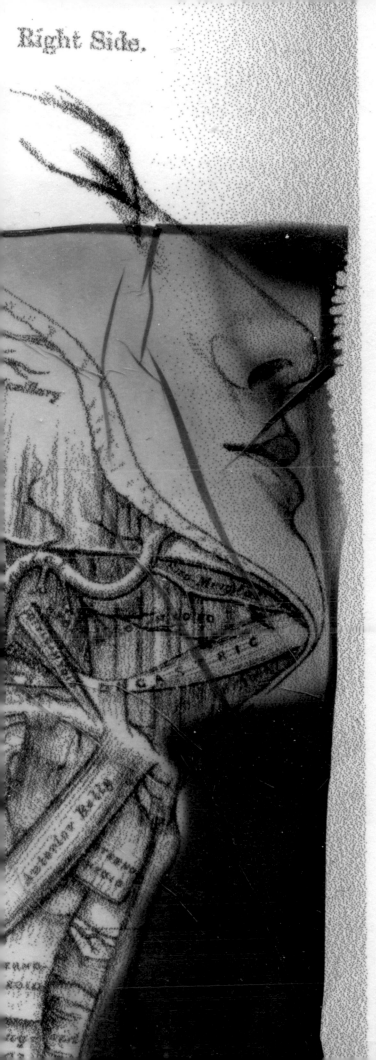

MARTIN CARTWRIGHT

**MARTIN CARTWRIGHT
UNITED KINGDOM**

**PX 600 SILVER
SHADE**

**CAMERA:
SPIRIT 600**

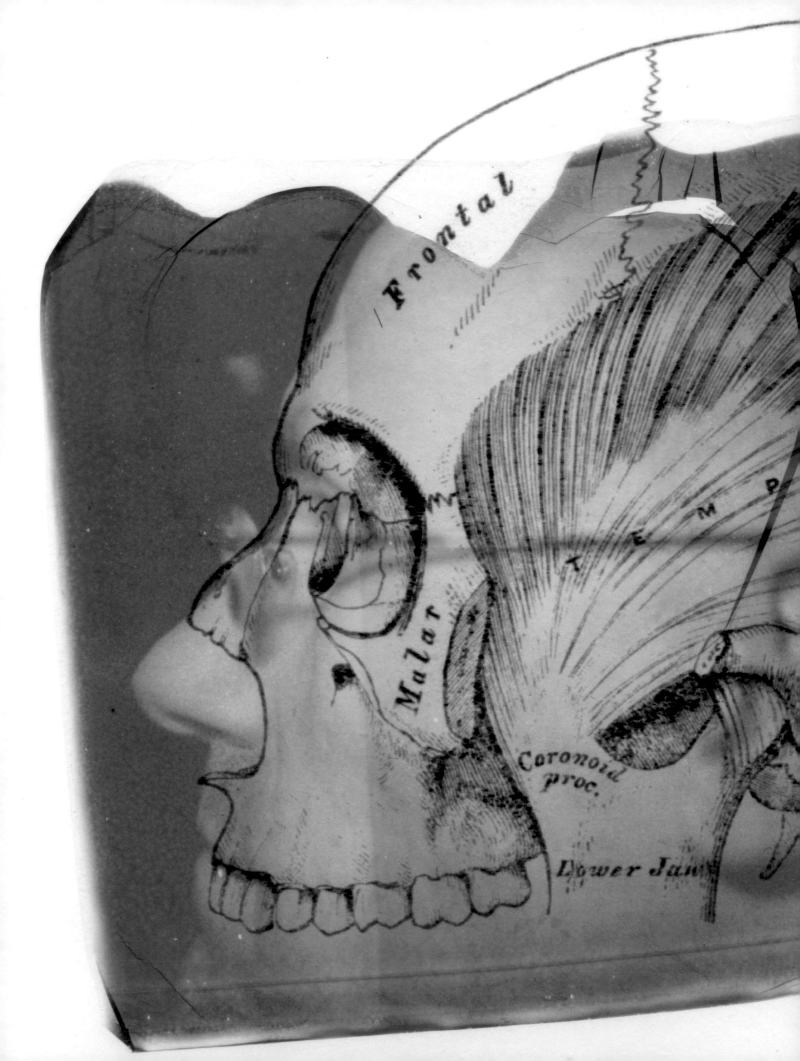

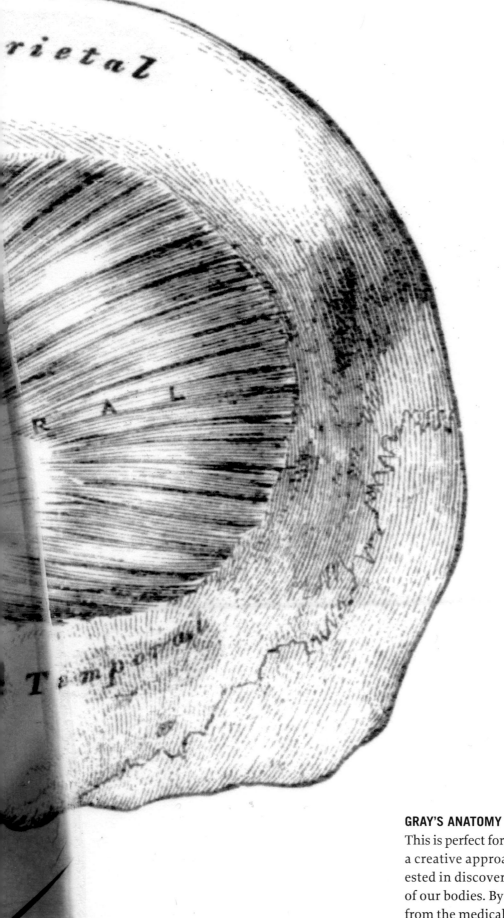

GRAY'S ANATOMY

This is perfect for medical students with a creative approach, or anyone interested in discovering the complexities of our bodies. By combining figures from the medical textbook Gray's Anatomy with emulsion lifts of Impossible photos, internal structure becomes visible in an unusual way.

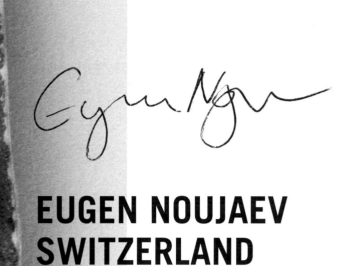

**EUGEN NOUJAEV
SWITZERLAND**

**PX 70 COLOR
SHADE**

**CAMERA:
SX 70 SONAR**

BAKING IMPOSSIBLE
The 3D technology of the 80s is experiencing a major boom, so I tried to push my Impossible photos in the same direction, but by different means. Heating the photos up deformed them and made various layers of the film visible. Their new cyberpunk look melted my heart.

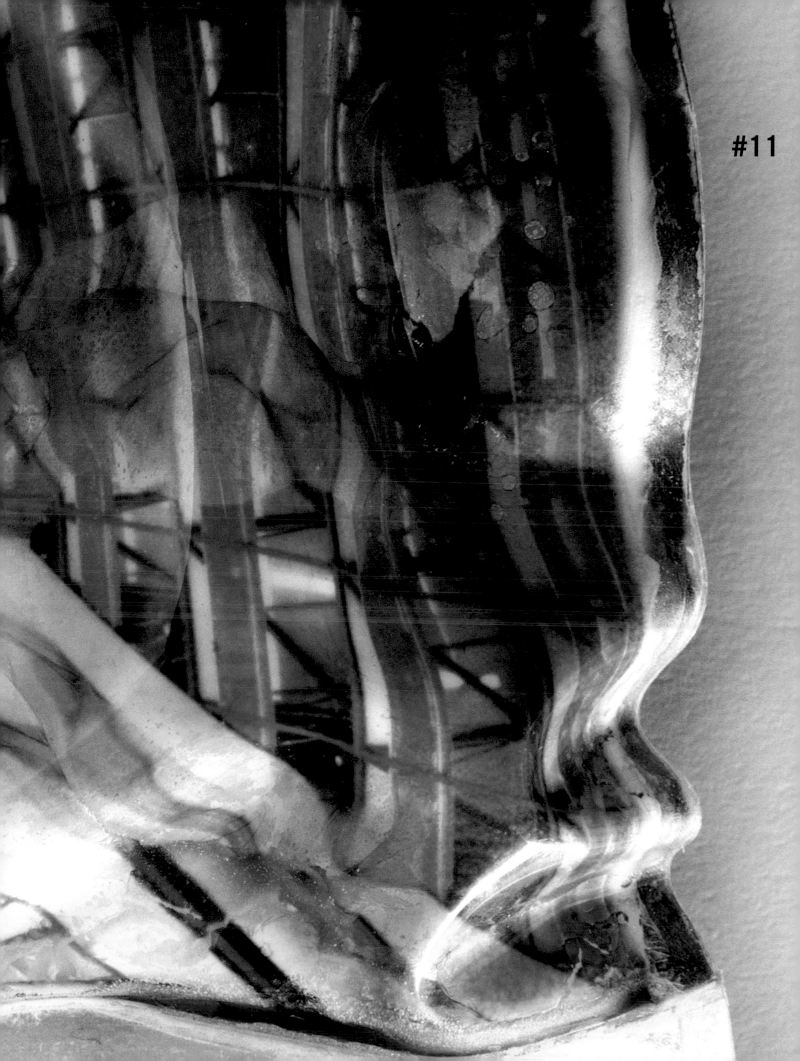

#11

franticham

**FRANTICHAM
IRELAND & SOUTH
KOREA**

**PX 70 COLOR
SHADE**

**CAMERAS:
SX 70
SX 70 SONAR**

10

대한민국 KOREA

대한민국 KOREA 900

here is t
n the glo
y challe
erely bo
Add to
aville Br
and the i
names'
and you
status q
designers
explore t
creativity
bid to mak
As Brod

aftern

12

DIARY FROM AN IMPOSSIBLE LOVE STORY
Francis from Ireland and Antic-Ham from Korea form a couple in life and work. Together, as franticham, they make artists' books and run Redfoxpress. During their time apart, they take Polaroid photographs and send them to each other as mail art collage postcards on a nearly daily basis.

sunshine ..

old house

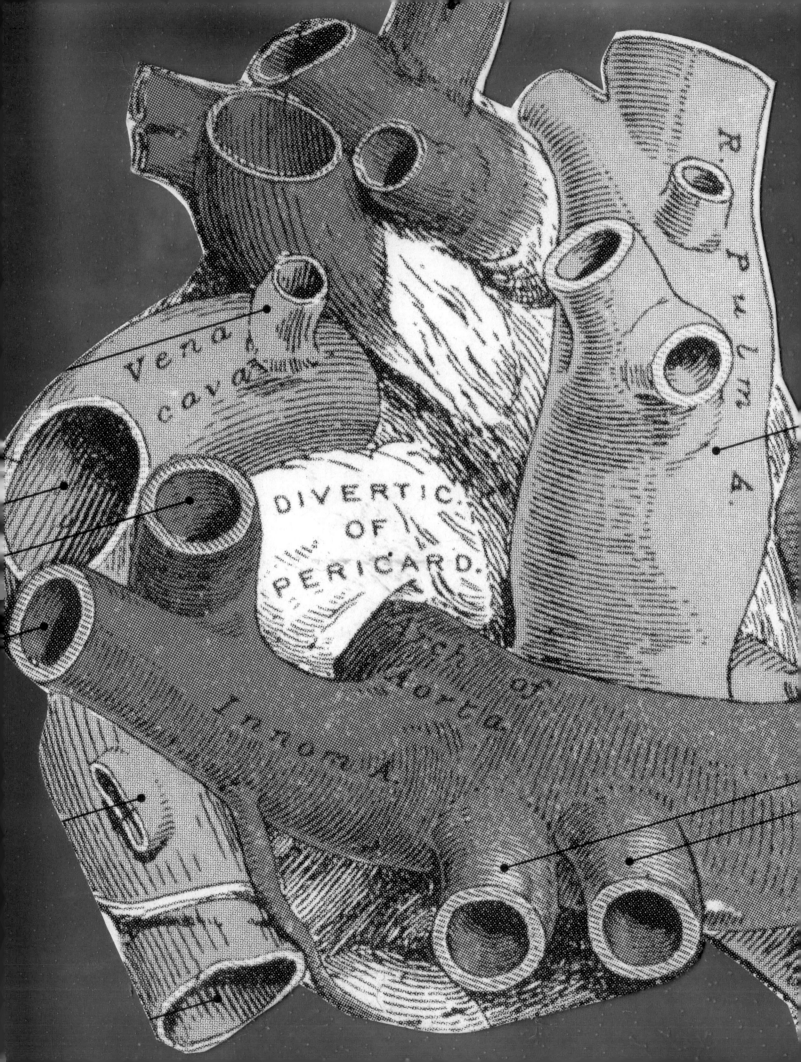

**EVER DUNDAS
SCOTLAND**

**PX 600 SILVER
SHADE**

**CAMERA:
600**

měr'ry a. joyous; ful[
slightly tipsy; **ma**
make fun of; ~
see -ITY)] foon
Chri'stie (k-) n
Chri'stmas (k
celebrated on
family reunic
man dresse

GREETING CARDS

I'm a collage artist, and when I became
addicted to Impossible films I knew
that I would incorporate them into my
collage work. Instead, they formed the
base for collage, and I use them to make
greeting cards for friends. This is a
particularly good project if you've been
experimenting with the film and the
photos haven't all worked out – you
don't feel like you're wasting the film,
as there's still a good use for them.

#13

onderland 513

3)

nderment 864 (1)

ondrous 864 (5)

ont 673 (1)

5 (4

ws 651 (

yea 488 (1)

year 108 (3)

IMPOSSIBLE DUCT TAPE DECORATION

Being a young photographer, I wanted
to make instant photography inspiring
for other kids my age, which meant I
needed something I could always have
around to show people. The idea was
to invent something mobile, a simple
way to have all of my photos with me
at all times. So I put them on a wallet.

14

Evan Cerda

EVAN CERDA
USA

PX 600 SILVER
SHADE BLACK
FRAME

CAMERA:
600

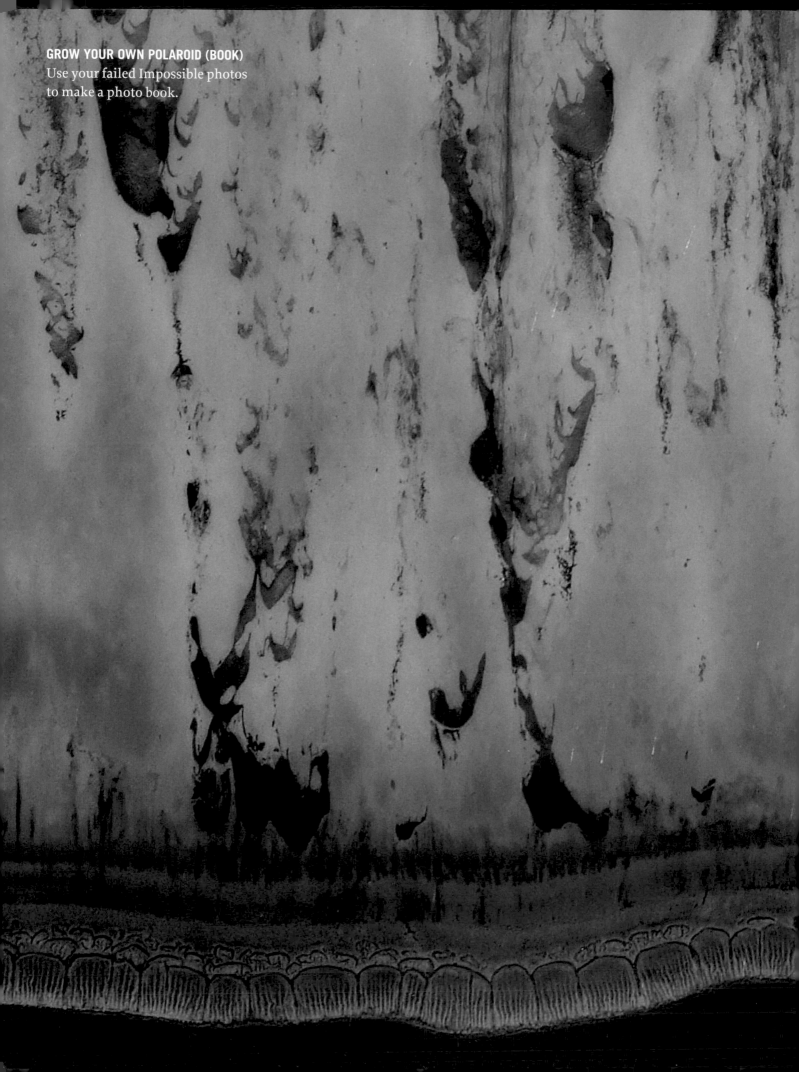

GROW YOUR OWN POLAROID (BOOK)
Use your failed Impossible photos
to make a photo book.

MELANIE J. ALEXANDROU

**MELANIE J. ALEXANDROU
ENGLAND**

**PZ 680 COLOR
SHADE**

**CAMERA:
POLAROID IMAGE 2**

MILK.

PAY BILLS.

EGGS.

IMPOSSIBLE REMINDER

Impossible-to-remember things are now impossible to forget, with this visual aid to your memory that can be of anything and go anywhere! It can be a reminder over breakfast in the kitchen or on the front door as a reminder on the way out.

16

BEN INNOCENT.

**BEN INNOCENT
ENGLAND**

**PX 680 COLOR
SHADE**

**CAMERA:
SX 70 SONAR WITH
ND FILTER**

GOUACHE + POLAROID

As an illustrator who lives in a house full of Polaroid cameras thanks to my boyfriend, I discovered that painting on the pictures was my favorite aspect of photography. I got out my gouache and added some birds around my dog's head by painting directly on the Impossible photo.

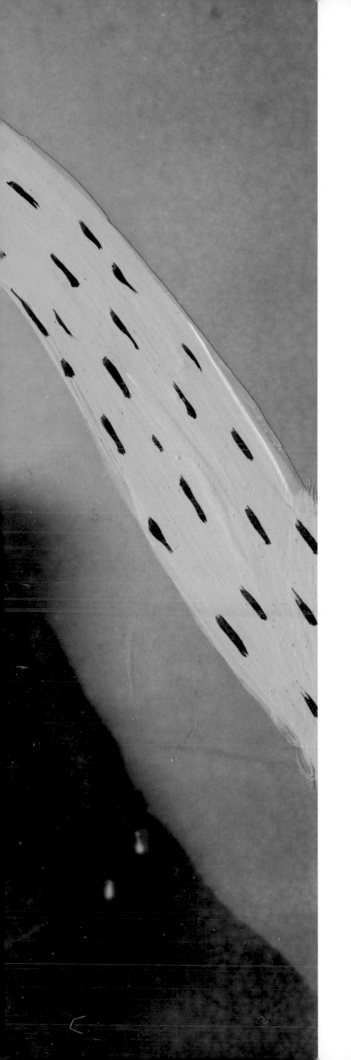

17

Roxanne Daner

**ROXANNE DANER
USA**

**PX 680 COLOR
SHADE**

**CAMERA:
ONE 600**

IMPOSSIBLE HIGH THICKNESS PHOTOS
I can't resist using different techniques in my creative work. I also have a weakness for three-dimensional effects. Applying colors and seeing them float on the photos makes me truly happy.

ALAN MARCHESELLI
ITALY

PX 600 SILVER
SHADE

PX 600 COLOR
SHADE

CAMERA:
ONE 600

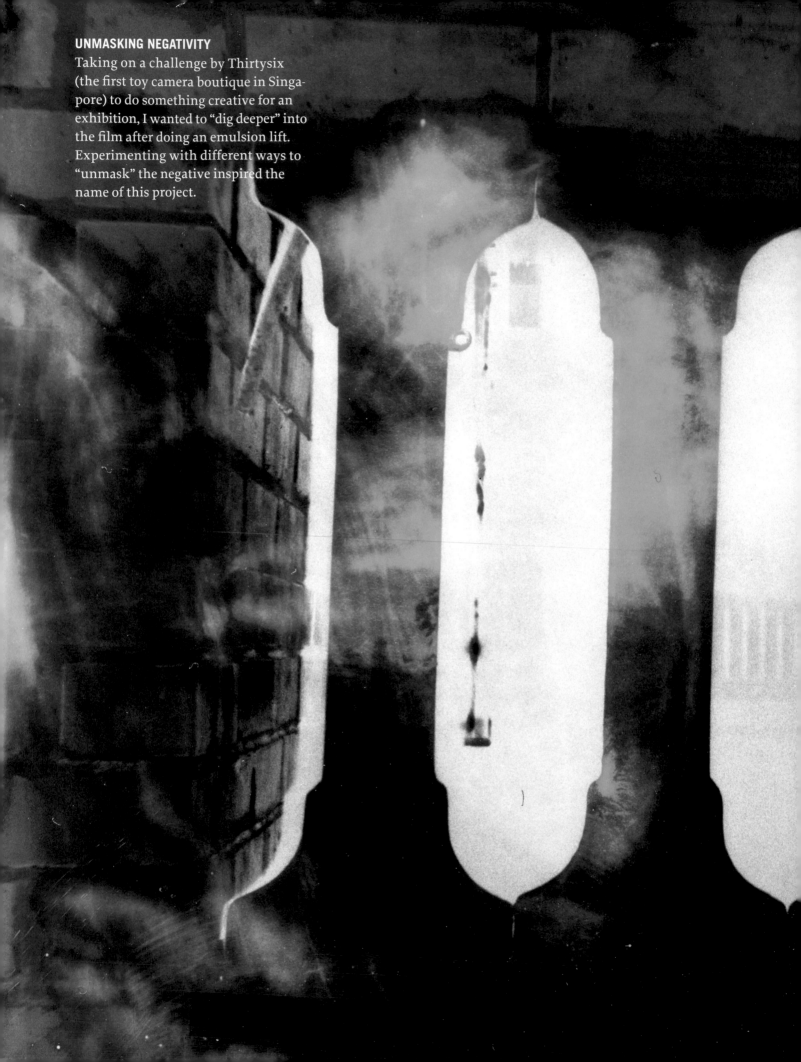

UNMASKING NEGATIVITY
Taking on a challenge by Thirtysix
(the first toy camera boutique in Singapore) to do something creative for an
exhibition, I wanted to "dig deeper" into
the film after doing an emulsion lift.
Experimenting with different ways to
"unmask" the negative inspired the
name of this project.

19

ANDREW KUA @ NDROO

**ANDREW KUA
SINGAPORE**

**PZ 680 COLOR
SHADE**

**CAMERA:
IMAGE SPECTRA**

2012

Impossible photos are magic. Even the ones that don't develop into a pretty picture. So why not turn them into a little art project and spread the message. Here I'm spreading love, peace and creativity for the new year.

Cécile de Vries

CÉCILE DE VRIES   #20
NETHERLANDS

PX 70 COLOR
SHADE

CAMERA:
SX 70 SONAR

0711448011   IMPOSSIBLE C!

www.the-impossible-project.com
keeping Polaroid cameras alive!

KEEP INSTANT

IMPOSSIBLE APOSTLE

A found Polaroid and childhood memory was enough to get me using instant film materials. In order to spread the mystery and wonder of instant film, I have left Impossible photos with messages on them in random places (or given them away), hoping to inspire and if nothing else to make someone smile.

KEEP INSTANT ALIVE

Ben Innocent.

**BEN INNOCENT
ENGLAND**

**PX 70 COLOR
SHADE**

**CAMERA:
SX 70**

ANT ALIVE

PX FILM AND MY SCANNER

Mix reality with what you just caught
on Impossible film to create unusual
visual impressions. I use Impossible
photos, any suitable objects and my
scanner to create these still life pictures.

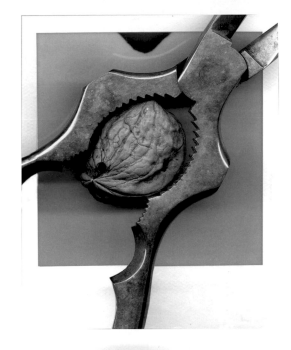

Bernd F. Oehmen #22

BERND F. OEHMEN
GERMANY

PX 70 COLOR
SHADE

CAMERA:
SX 70

IMPOSSIBLE SUN PRINT
For a stunning visual effect, use an
Impossible transparency to create a
picture on sun print paper.

#23

Britta Hershman

**BRITTA HERSHMAN
USA**

**PX 100 SILVER
SHADE**

**CAMERA:
SX 70**

INVADING LEGO WORLD WITH IMPOSSIBLES

A small photo for a human being is an enormous shot for Lego people. Present Impossible masterpieces as if they were in a museum. The Lego world is funny, the Lego world is intelligent, the Lego world is brilliant, the Lego world is life!

24

Fieni Enrico

**ENRICO FIENI
ITALY**

**PX 70 COLOR
SHADE**

**CAMERA:
SX 70 SONAR**

IMPOSSIBLE BOOKPLATES

Here's a use for those photos that didn't quite turn out right. Make your own Impossible bookplates and stamp some instant love onto your favorite books before sharing them with your friends. It's a nice reminder to everyone that instant photography isn't dead and neither is the printed page.

Candice Morato

25

**CANDICE MORATO
AUSTRALIA**

**PX 680 COLOR
SHADE FF**

**CAMERA:
ONESTEP EXPRESS
600**

TYPEWRITER

They say a picture paints a thousand
words, but some words always jump
out more than others. By typing on my
pictures, I am able to tell people what
they mean specifically to me. I can title
and sign my photos, interpret them,
share a memory, show a feeling or add
to the story they represent.

Eliza Agosta

ELIZA AGOSTA
USA

PX 680 COLOR
SHADE

CAMERA:
SLR 680

IMPOSSIBLE LOVE

Is this burning an eternal flame? Does
love last forever? Some people say
nothing lasts forever. Is it impossible?
It is (not) – in this project about love,
kisses and Impossible.

**ERIK SOSSO
ITALY**

**PZ 680 COLOR
SHADE**

**CAMERA:
IMAGE/SPECTRA PRO**

TRANSFER ONTO AN OBJECT
To raise my photos out of their flatness, I transferred them onto a Styrofoam ball. Then I again captured the ball with a Polaroid SLR 680 camera, using PX 600 UV+ film. For beginners I recommend using Color Shade films, as they are much sturdier.

Ferdinand Vykoukal

FERDINAND VYKOUKAL
SPAIN
#28

PX 70 COLOR
SHADE

CAMERA:
1000

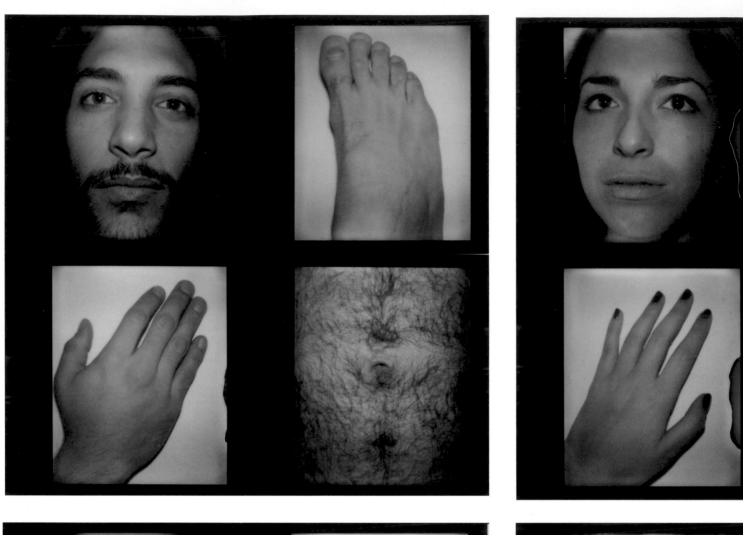

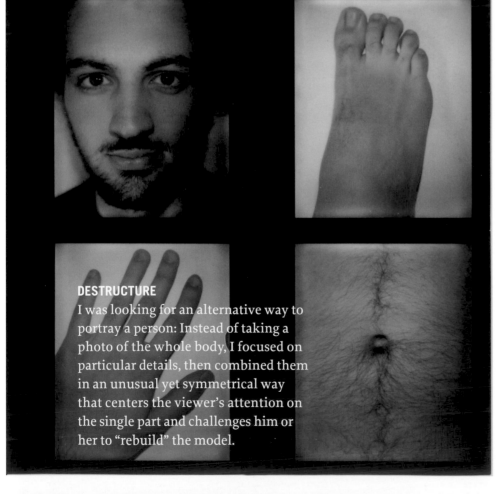

DESTRUCTURE
I was looking for an alternative way to portray a person: Instead of taking a photo of the whole body, I focused on particular details, then combined them in an unusual yet symmetrical way that centers the viewer's attention on the single part and challenges him or her to "rebuild" the model.

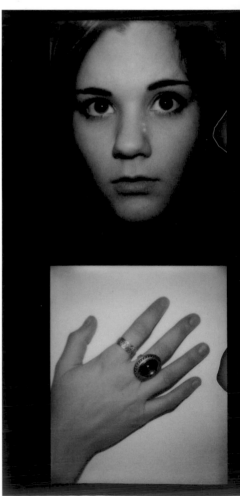

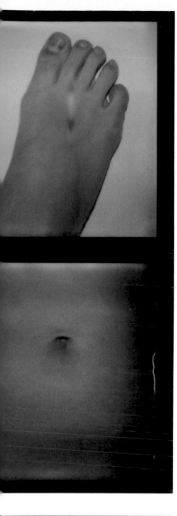

GABRIELE PAGANI
ITALY

#29

PZ 600 SILVER SHADE BLACK FRAME

CAMERA: POLAROID IMAGE SYSTEM

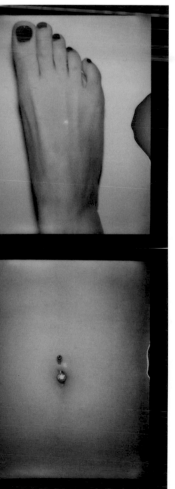

Change your vision by placing clear textured glass in front of your Polaroid camera's lens. When you like what you see, take a picture and discover an altered reality.

Genevieve Neal

GENEVIEVE NEAL
USA

#30

PX 600 SILVER
SHADE

CAMERA:
600

HALF COLOR, HALF MONOCHROME
If you're not the either/or type, create photos that are half color, half black and white – make a film cartridge that shoots two types of film.

31

IGNAS KUTAVIČIUS

**IGNAS KUTAVICIUS
LITHUANIA**

**PX 600 SILVER
SHADE**

**PX 680 COLOR
SHADE**

**CAMERA:
600**

THE IMPOSSIBLE LAMP
Sometimes simple does it: an emulsion lift, a sandwich bag and a candle. That's all you need to create your romantic lamp and light up your life.

Ina Echternach

#32

INA ECHTERNACH
GERMANY

PX 70 COLOR
SHADE

CAMERA:
SX 70

IMPOSSIBLE HEAT

You can achieve an amazing effect by heating developing PX 100 Silver Shade film with short bursts from a hairdryer. Cover up the lighter parts of the photo and work around them to maximize the contrasting solarization and the impact of the final picture.

James Matthew Carroll

JAMES MATTHEW CARROLL
UNITED KINGDOM   #33

PX 100 SILVER
SHADE

CAMERA:
SX 70 SONAR

ME, MYSELF AND I

All memories are fake – as soon as they're recorded in the brain, they become kind of a lie. That's why I like saving certain moments in a photo. This poster is a way to preserve and remember important moments. My family, my friends, my things – this Impossible project is all about me and my life.

JOSEAN MOLINA
SPAIN

PX 70 COLOR
SHADE

CAMERA:
SX 70

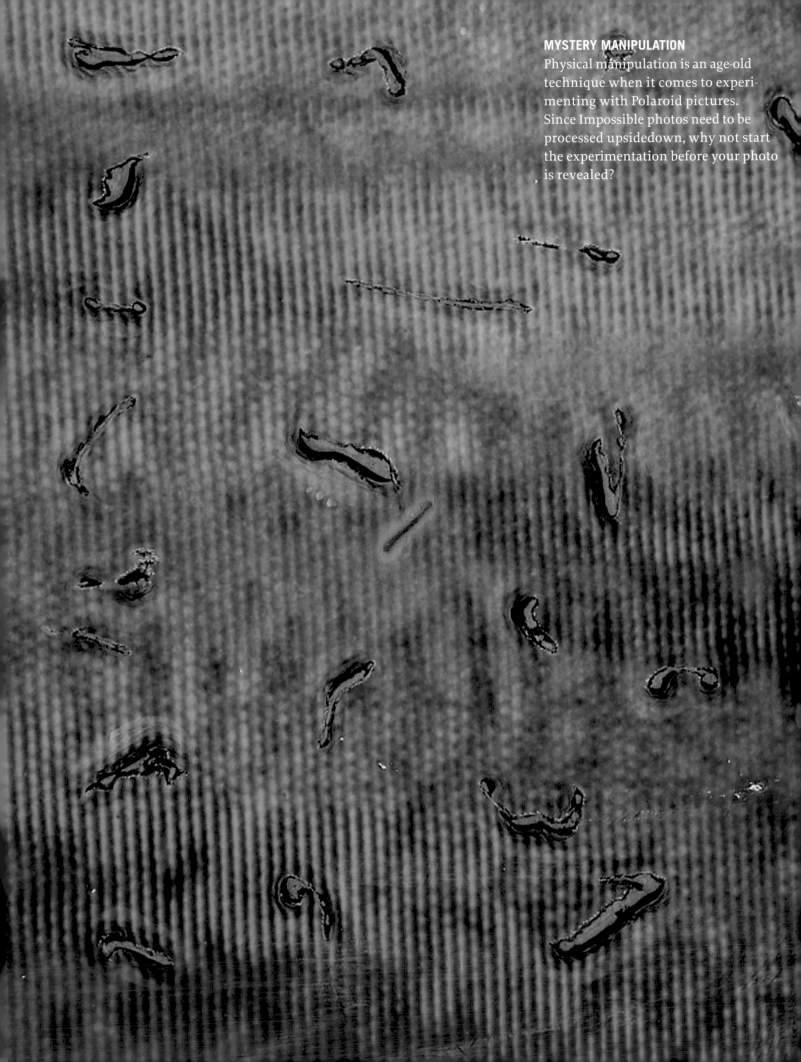

MYSTERY MANIPULATION
Physical manipulation is an age-old
technique when it comes to experimenting with Polaroid pictures.
Since Impossible photos need to be
processed upsidedown, why not start
the experimentation before your photo
is revealed?

#35

Jonathan Campolo

JONATHAN CAMPOLO
USA

PZ 680 COLOR
SHADE

CAMERA:
MINOLTA PRO

WEAR AN IMPOSSIBLE DRESS
What I see becomes my dress, so I
can carry my favorite photos with
me and on me all the time.

CHIHARU HOSHIDA

**CHIHARU HOSHIDA
JAPAN**

#36

**PX 70 COLOR
SHADE**

**PX 680 COLOR
SHADE**

**CAMERAS:
SX 70
SLR 680**

MULTI-SHOT PORTRAIT
Make a portrait from several Impossible
film shots.

IGNAS KUTAVIČIUS

IGNAS KUTAVICIUS
LITHUANIA

PX 600 SILVER
SHADE UV+ BLACK
FRAME

CAMERA:
SX 70 WITH
ND FILTER

#37

Katie Sykes

KATIE SYKES
USA

PX 70 COLOR
SHADE

#38

CAMERA:
SX 70 SONAR

ADDRESSES ARE COOL
I love capturing interesting things on
my daily commute. I started noticing
addresses and have been shooting them
ever since. This project is really all
about finding beauty in the mundane.

ARRANGING BOOKS IN
AN IMPOSSIBLE WAY

My way of having my favorite Impossible photos in my room as both decoration and practical device. A very simple idea, but because of the indefinable magic Impossible photos convey, even this simple idea has an incredibly aesthetic force.

Lena Louisa Burggraef

LENA BURGGRAEF
GERMANY

PX 600 SILVER SHADE UV+ BLACK FRAME

PX 600 SILVER SHADE UV+

CAMERA: POLAROID SPIRIT 600 CL

#39

DOUBLE EXPOSURE

The charm of Impossible lies in the unexpected results, the anticipation of what's to come after you press the button. Shooting with Impossible film is even more fun when shooting double (multiple) exposures.

Frank Brouwer

**FRANK BROUWER
NETHERLANDS**

**PZ 680 COLOR
SHADE**

**CAMERA: #40
IMAGE/SPECTRA**

PICTURE STORY – LITTLE ACHI'S LIONS
Here I've tried to combine two of my passions, my son and instant photography. Flipping through an old newspaper found in my grandmother's attic, I was surprised to see the picture stories that were once so popular and thought of creating something similar.

Federico Corpieri (signature)

**FEDERICO CORPIERI
ITALY**

**PX 680 COLOR
SHADE**

**CAMERA:
SLR 680**

BRING YOUR IMPOSSIBLES EVERYWHERE
Carry your favorite photos with you
and hang them everywhere! You can
even create a temporary mini display
of Impossible art wherever you go.
With just an empty Impossible battery
and a paperclip, carry virtually infinite
food for your imagination and never feel
far from where you belong.

Mariadonata

**MARIADONATA VILLA
ITALY**

**PX 600 SILVER
SHADE**

#42

**PX 680 COLOR
SHADE**

**CAMERA:
600**

MY IMPOSSIBLE HERBARIUM
Just like nature's gifts, every instant
photo is precious. I keep my favorite
flowers from my garden inside PX 70
photos, then collect all of them in a note-
book to create my precious "Impossible
Herbarium."

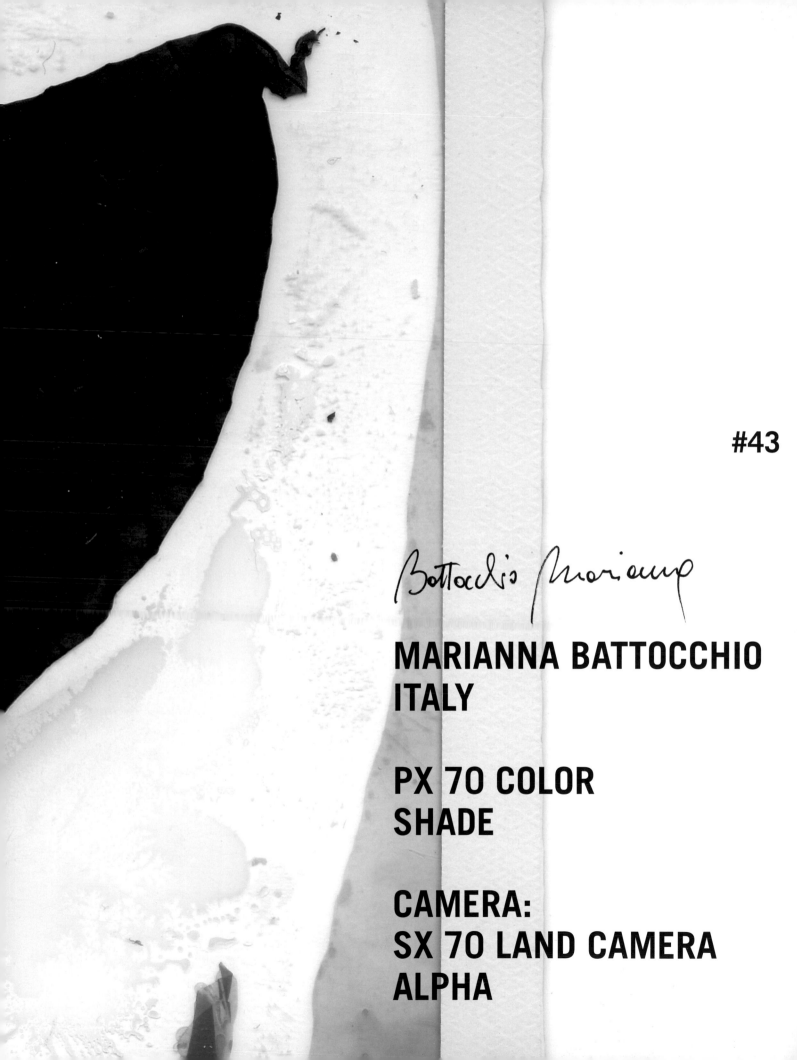

#43

MARIANNA BATTOCCHIO
ITALY

PX 70 COLOR
SHADE

CAMERA:
SX 70 LAND CAMERA
ALPHA

IMPOSSIBLE YEAR

An Impossible Year never ends and the
story continues with Impossible films.
Mix and match your current month
with photos of your favorite memories.
Recall them by simply flipping the pages
of your calendar.

Dorota Wagner (signature)

**DOROTA WAGNER
POLAND**

**PX 680 COLOR
SHADE**

**PX 70 COLOR
SHADE**

#44

**CAMERAS:
SX 70
600**

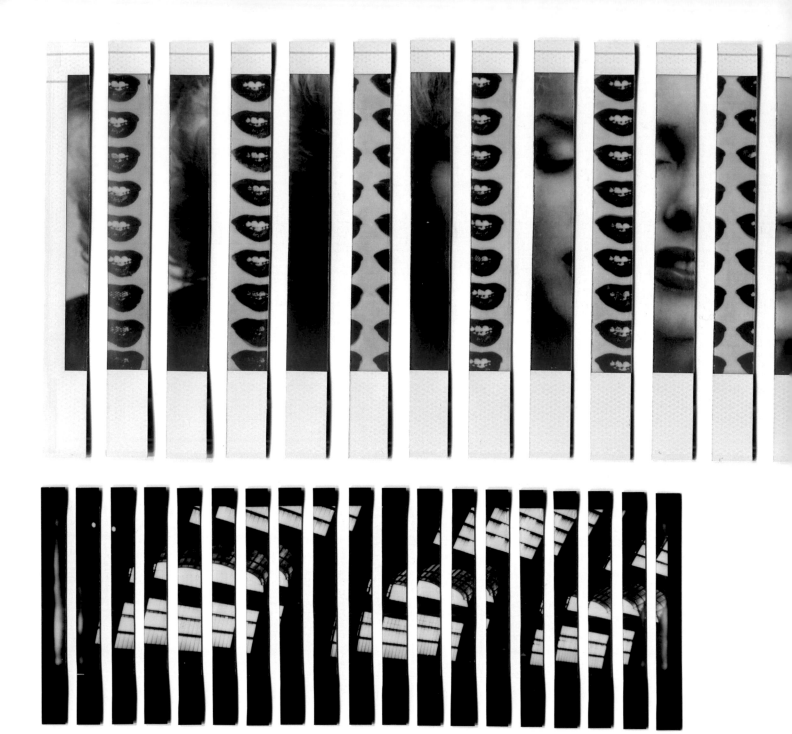

(S)COMPOSITE
Cutting material as practiced by Fontana and in genius compositions by Hockney and Galimberti: The alchemy of these elements gave birth to the idea of using instant photography in a completely new and different way.

#45

MASSIMILIANO MUNER
ITALY

PZ 600 SILVER
SHADE BLACK FRAME

PZ 680 COLOR
SHADE

CAMERA:
IMAGE/SPECTRA

A TRIBUTE TO ALFRED HITCHCOCK
A whole movie in just 3 Impossible
photos.

MASSIMO BATTISTA
ITALY

#46

PZ 600 SILVER
SHADE BLACK FRAME

CAMERA:
IMAGE/SPECTRA

DO YOU BELIEVE IN NEGATIVE?

I'm in love with emulsions, but was always hesitant to throw the rest of the photo away, as I couldn't believe it was meant for the trash. During a workshop I gave on emulsions, I soaked the white unused side of the photo in hot water and obtained a magic "negative" to preserve and use!

MICHELA SCAGNETTI
ITALY

PX 600 SILVER
SHADE UV+

CAMERA:
636 CLOSE-UP   #47

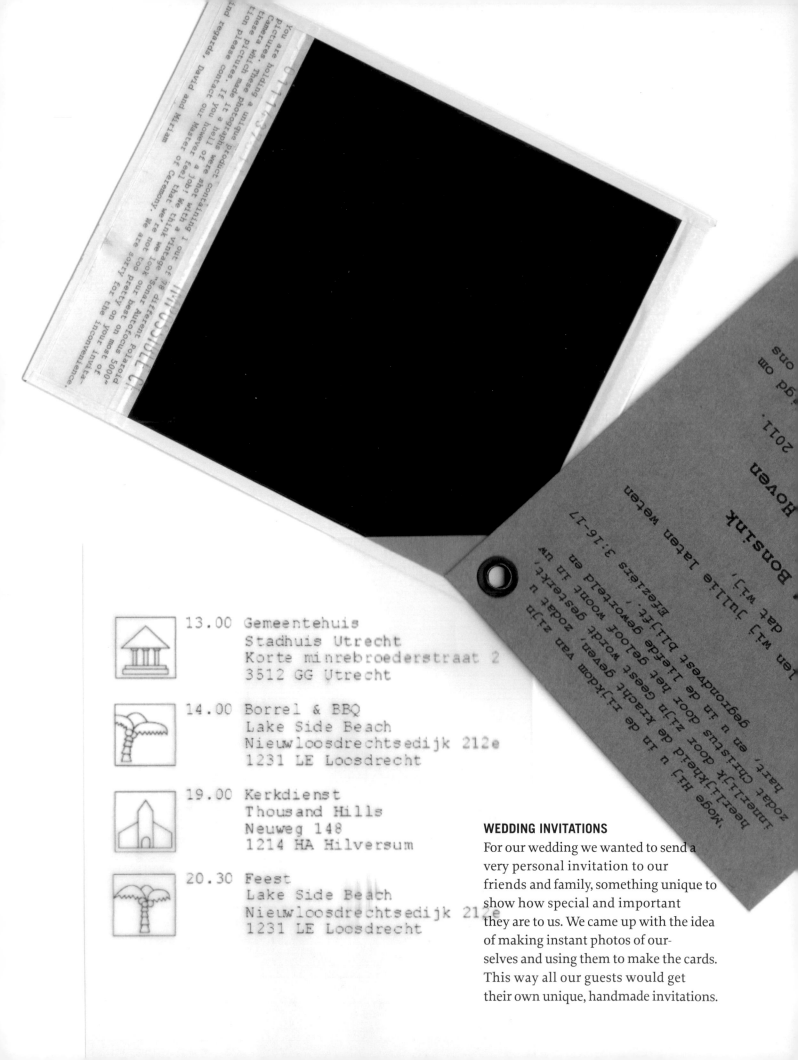

Left schedule card:

13.00 Gemeentehuis
Stadhuis Utrecht
Korte minrebroederstraat 2
3512 GG Utrecht

14.00 Borrel & BBQ
Lake Side Beach
Nieuwloosdrechtsedijk 212e
1231 LE Loosdrecht

19.00 Kerkdienst
Thousand Hills
Neuweg 148
1214 HA Hilversum

20.30 Feest
Lake Side Beach
Nieuwloosdrechtsedijk 212e
1231 LE Loosdrecht

Polaroid sleeve text:

You are holding pictures. Camera's these which tion picture please... These a unique photographs made product it a graphs which were containing that we think 1 out of 78 different Vintage. We look Sonar of that we feel job! with a shot however of a look our best Autofocus Polaroid pretty on most 5000w our Master feel Job! of Ceremony. We are not too sorry for on your invites- contact you hell were and regards, David and Miriam the inconvenience.

Right card (Dutch):

Moge Hij u in de rijkdom van zijn heerlijkheid de kracht geven door zijn Geest uw innerlijke mens te versterken, zodat Christus door het geloof woont in uw hart, en u in de liefde geworteld en gegrondvest blijkt. Efeziers 3:16-17

... dat jullie laten weten ... Bonsink ... hoven ... 2011.

WEDDING INVITATIONS

For our wedding we wanted to send a very personal invitation to our friends and family, something unique to show how special and important they are to us. We came up with the idea of making instant photos of ourselves and using them to make the cards. This way all our guests would get their own unique, handmade invitations.

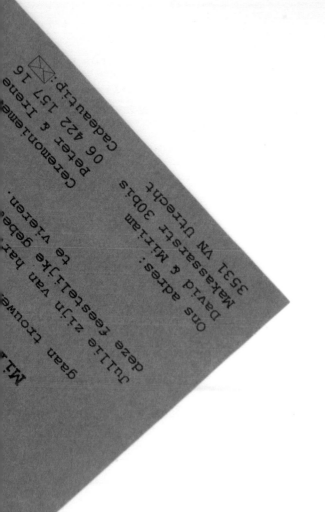

Miriam van Hoven

**MIRIAM VAN HOVEN
NETHERLANDS**

**PX 70 COLOR
SHADE**

**CAMERA:
SX 70 SONAR**

AIR MOBILE
Inspired by Alexander Calder's delicate
mobiles, I created this airplane mobile
built with Impossible integral instant
photos. To add a much lighter look to
your construction you can also use
transparencies.

Nuno Tudela

**NUNO TUDELA
PORTUGAL**

PX 680 COLOR   **#49**
SHADE

**CAMERA:
SX 70 ALPHA 1
WITH ND FILTER**

BEWARE
OF HIGH CONTRASTED
SCENE

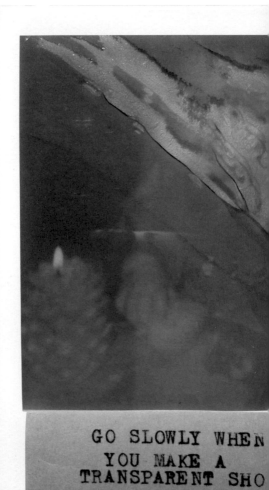

GO SLOWLY WHEN
YOU MAKE A
TRANSPARENT SHO

USER MANUAL FOR BEGINNERS

This is an Impossible manual for newbies. Are you tired of seeing your photos ruined? Wrong light, wrong subject, not in focus, bad shielding, wrong film, etc.? Don't get rid of these photos, but make an album out of them. Learn from mistakes, stay tuned, avoid simple mistakes and take better photos.

Rudy Force

**RUDY FORCE
FRANCE**

**PX 70 COLOR
SHADE**

**CAMERAS:
SX 70 SONAR
600**

#50

ON-OFF-ON-OFF
I created this lamp out of a passion
for individual furnishings and a wish to
admire my Impossible photos in an
unusual way. It not only illuminates
your transparencies, but can also radiate
a message.

giovanna

**GIOVANNA CHEMI
ITALY** #51

**PX 600 SILVER
SHADE**

**CAMERA:
600**

IMꝗOSSIBLE · MEMORY

IMPOSSIBLE MEMORY

Have you ever experienced a hard-won
victory against a child in a memory
game? This instant version of integrated
memory training has been developed
to help you train for precisely this. Carefully shoot two Impossible photos of
the same subject and practice every day.

Sebastian "Ambigu MC" Gulak

SEBASTIAN GULAK
GERMANY

PX 680 SILVER
SHADE

CAMERA:
600 ROUND TOP
GRAY   #52

MEMORY IN POLAROID

I wanted to chronicle the important events, people and inspirations in my life with my Impossible photos. The classic beauty of the white frame allowed me to enhance my memory of those moments using Sharpies, paints and any materials imaginable, extending the image beyond the usual borders of its frame.

TAYLOR SHURTE

TAYLOR SHURTE
USA

PX 680 COLOR
SHADE

#53

CAMERAS:
SX 70
600
WITH ND FILTER

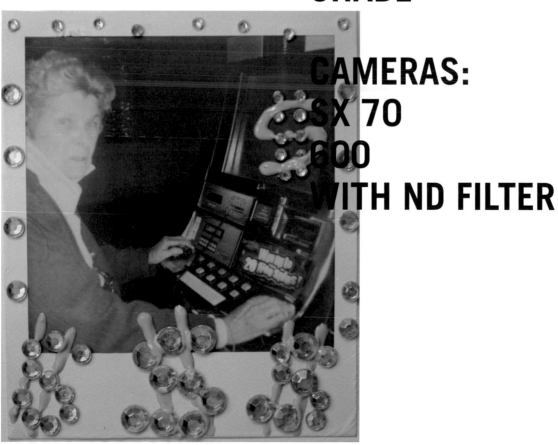

PEEL & PRESS IT

I was searching for a maximum degree of distortion that would give my pictures an enhanced feeling of abstraction, but with the frame remaining to provide the familiar integral film look.
In the end, I pulled the back and front layer apart and then pushed them back together immediately afterward.

Von Koreander

**TUNG CHU
GERMANY**

**PX 70 COLOR
SHADE**

#54

**CAMERA:
SX 70 MODEL 2**

I was looking for a way to use photos that didn't expose correctly. It seemed like such a waste to just throw them away. So I decided to tear them apart and use tools to create some simple line drawings.

#55

Thomas Gallagher

**TOM GALLAGHER
USA**

**PX 100 SILVER
SHADE**

**CAMERA:
SX 70**

HIDDEN TREASURES

In "Hidden Treasures," an old book
becomes a vessel to conceal a treasure.
Instead of an object, the book's secret
compartment holds a photograph, a
document of someone's special trinket.
The cover hints at what's inside.

Susanna Gaunt

**SUSANNA GAUNT
USA**

**PX 70 COLOR
SHADE PUSH!**

#56

**CAMERA:
SX 70 SONAR**

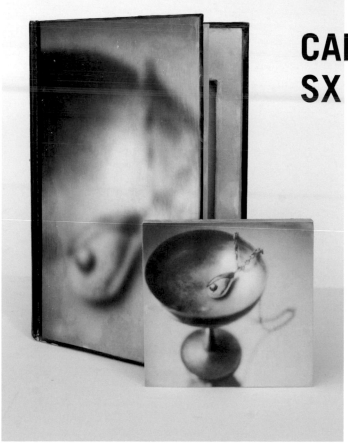

CREATING MY OWN REALITY

Sometimes I very much feel like creating my own reality. As this is impossible, I try to capture my ideas and desires in my photos. I like instant photography because of its simplicity and non-digital character, so I looked for ways to edit my pictures and create my own reality without using any digital methods.

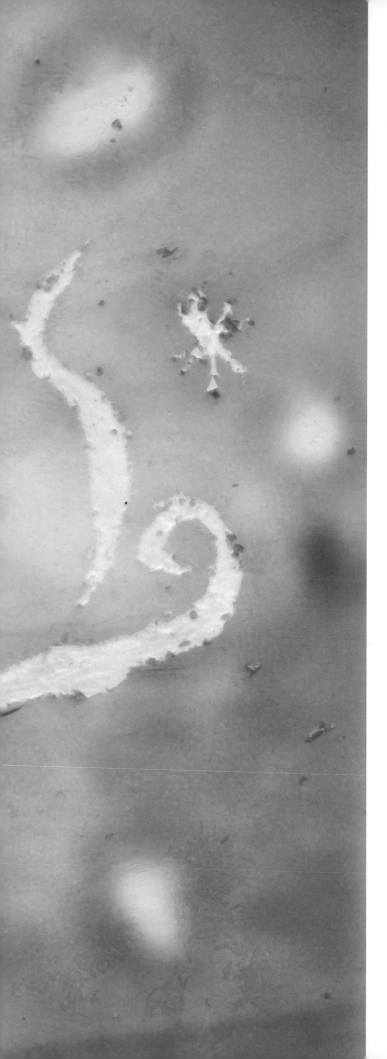

Doreen Stahr

DOREEN STAHR
GERMANY

PX 600 SILVER
SHADE

CAMERA:
SX 70
WITH ND FILTER

#57

TOBIAS' PHOTO BOX
We love photo booths. We love
Impossible. So why not combine
both and create an "Impossible
photo booth," or as we call it
"Tobias' photo box" (named after
our lively young muse).

TOBIAS, ANNE
ASCHENBRENNER
AND CLAUDIA MENG
AUSTRIA

PX 600 SILVER
SHADE GREY FRAME   #58

PX 680 COLOR
SHADE

CAMERA:
SLR 680

ON THE ROAD

This is for people who spend a lot of time in the car and/or in hotel rooms, such as taxi/truck drivers, sales agents, managers/consultants or engineers. Use your Impossible frame in the car and on your hotel bedside table for your personal "Impossible Car/Traveling Picture Frame."

**THOMAS HOFMANN
AUSTRIA**

#59

**PX 600 SILVER
SHADE UV+ BLACK
FRAME**

**CAMERA:
SX 70 SONAR POLA-
SONIC MODEL 2
WITH ND FILTER**

A UNIQUE CLOCK
Just like instant photography, time
is one of the most valuable things in
an analog life. With my unique clock,
I bring both of them together.

CHRISTIAN DYLONG
GERMANY

PX 70 COLOR
SHADE

CAMERA:
SX 70

#60

On the image:

19

Boxes of Polaroids used since January 1, 2011.

Day Eighty Two:
(March 23, 2011)

PX-70 First Flush.

It was cold out today. the sun was decieving. looking out of the window. I thought it would be much warmer outside than what it was. I captured this image using the natural light in the spare room. I love the turquoise wall and the white door. My camera has started leaving it's "fingerprint" at the top of some images. I'm told that the SX-70 cameras start to do this over time. it doesn't bother me though, it seems to give the Polaroids personality.

IMPOSSIBLE POP-UP

I wanted a way to store and document my favorite Impossible photos, with the goal of turning them into a book the user interacts with. The idea was that Polaroid cameras and Impossible film demand user interaction, so it seemed fitting for the book to do the same.

Sarah Crookston

SARAH CROOKSTON
USA   #61

PX 600 SILVER
SHADE BLACK FRAME

PX 70 COLOR
SHADE

CAMERA:
SX 70 SONAR

www.the-impossible-project.com
www.the-impossible-project.com
www.the-impossible-project.com
www.the-impossible-project.com
www.the-impossible-project.com
www.the-impossible-project.com
www.the-impossible-project.com
www.the-impossible-project.com
www.the-impossible-project.com

ADVERTISE
Use Impossible film to advertise something on the streets. Advertise your webpage, something you want to sell or Impossible film itself! Spread the word and share the love!

IGNAS KUTAVIČIUS

**IGNAS KUTAVICIUS
LITHUANIA**

**PX 100 SILVER
SHADE**

**CAMERA:
SX 70**

#62

OBSERVER/PARTICIPANT

Inspired by "The Memory of Water" by Masaru Emoto and by Fugazi's song "Ex-Spectator," I started working on a series of portraits that viewers would alter with their own reflection. Impossible transparencies are attached to a mirror, and the viewer's reflection modifies the portrait and becomes part of the result.

Böiter

MIK BOITIER
ITALY

PX 600 SILVER
~~SH~~ADE BLACK

CAMERA:
SLR 680 WITH
CLOSE-UP LENSES

#63

VIVID POSTCARDS

They say sending postcards is a dying art. But they also said that about analog instant photography. My project makes both of these as alive as it gets. Stamp and address your photo, post it and let it travel the world, touching people and places, carrying your life to the ones you want to share it with.

EUROPE

Claudia Meng

CLAUDIA MENG
AUSTRIA

PX 680 COLOR
SHADE

CAMERAS:
SLR 680

#64

LEARN A LANGUAGE
Learn a new word a day. Learning a language is a cumulative process. If you don't use it, you forget it. This project provides a visually engaging way to commit to learning a language ... even if it's just one word a day!

"Candies"

Italiano : caramelle

日本語 : キャンディー

한국어 : 캔디

Française : les bonbons

Dansk : slik

Čestina : bonbony

Italiano: Felice San Valentino!
日本語：ハッピーバレンタインデー！
한국어: 행복한 발렌타인 데이!

orchid • orchidèe • 난초 • orchidea

deborah yun

**DEBORAH YUN
USA**

**PX 680 COLOR
SHADE**

**CAMERA:
POLAROID IMPULSE**

#65

HIGH KEY
It all started with an experiment in copying a lantern slide directly onto an integral instant photo. I used an overexposed PX film sheet as a working basis and added different objects. This allowed me to create still lifes that show two layers in one photo.

Bernd F. Oehmen (signature)

**BERND F. OEHMEN
GERMANY**

**PX 100 SILVER
SHADE**

**CAMERA:
SX 70**   **#66**

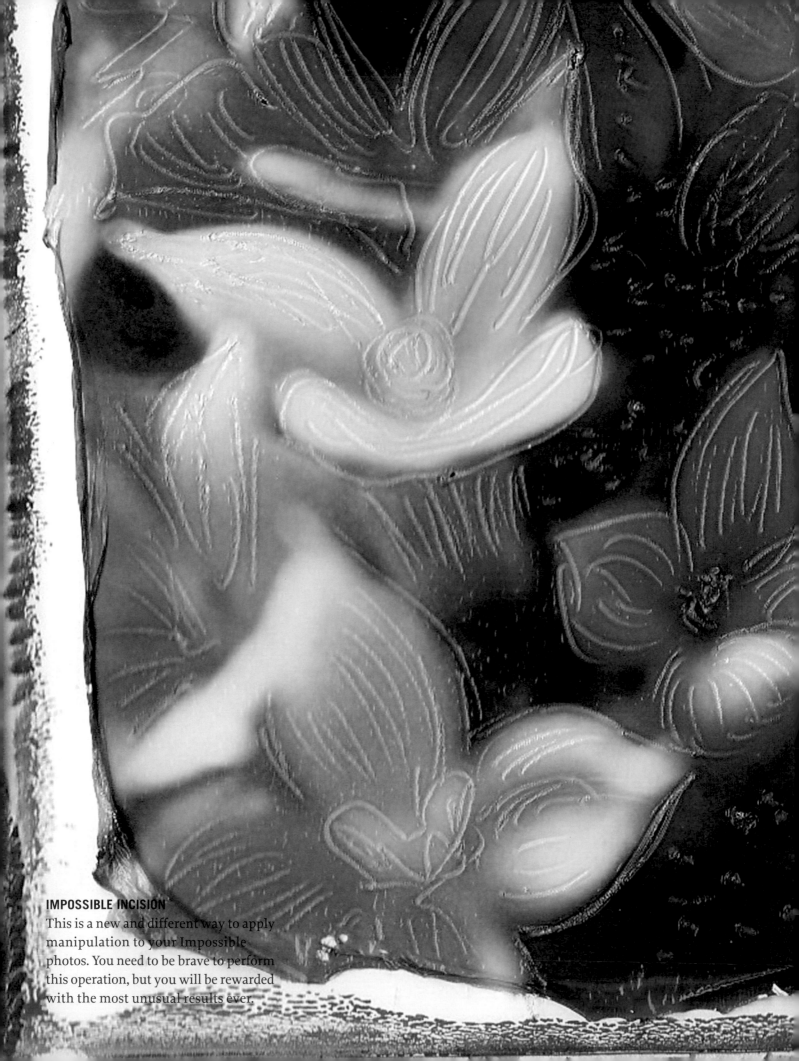

IMPOSSIBLE INCISION

This is a new and different way to apply manipulation to your Impossible photos. You need to be brave to perform this operation, but you will be rewarded with the most unusual results ever.

CARMEN PALERMO
ITALY

PX 680 COLOR
SHADE

CAMERA:
600

#67

Very dear friends were getting married.
The question was, what could we
possibly give them as a personal gift to
remember?
We ended up producing an Impossible
instant film guest book of the wedding in
an instant – well, in just the time from
the beginning to the end of the party.

ANDREAS SCHIMANSKI
GERMANY

PX 600 SILVER
SHADE

PX 680 COLOR
SHADE

CAMERA:
POLAROID 636
CLOSE-UP

#68

INNER LIFE

An instant photo is more than just a photo. There is much more behind it, something magic, an inner life. This is what I wanted to show in my project: The photo is not just the result of a pure chemical process, but is made with feelings, and has a heart and a soul to be discovered.

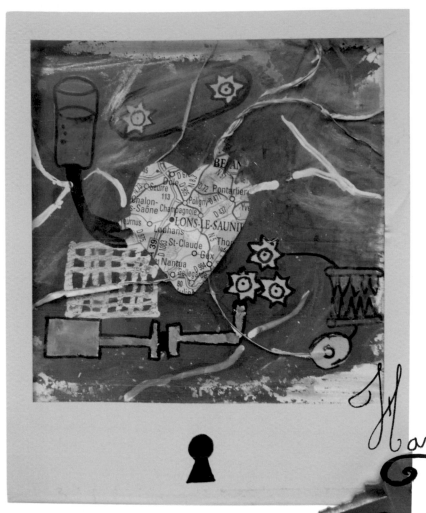

Hannah Doucet

HANNAH DOUCET
FRANCE

#69

PX 100 SILVER
SHADE

CAMERA:
SX 70 SONAR

In our place
we find what
we are.

GB4

DAILY VISUAL MEDITATION

I love associating images with words –
it stimulates the imagination, creates
stories, evokes memories and reso-
nances. Every little thing on this planet
has the power to illustrate the quote
of a great mind – let's capture it on
Impossible film! The quotes I use all
come from Yogi Tea tags.

Learn to appreciate yourself.
GB4

Together we can do what we never can do alone.
GB4

Emilie Le Fellic

**EMILIE LEFELLIC
FRANCE**

**PX 680 COLOR
SHADE**

#70

**CAMERA:
SX 70
WITH ND FILTER**

THE GIANT TRIPTYCH
IMPOSSIBLE PROJECT

Use not one but three photos to take a portrait! The head, torso and feet capture the person's essence. This project of mine has been going on for some time and recently I created a Life Size Impossible Portrait Exhibit for a New York gallery.

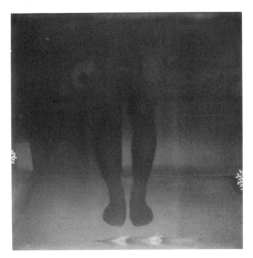

**REMO CAMEROTA
USA**

**PX 70 COLOR
SHADE**

**PZ 680 COLOR
SHADE**

#71

**CAMERAS:
SX 70 SONAR
IMAGE/SPECTRA**

REFRIGERATOR FUN

I love watching people interact, especially when I can't hear what they're saying. Facial expressions and body language are interesting out of context. I thought it would be fun to recreate that interaction with Impossible photos, each one representing a person – in this case my mom and dad.

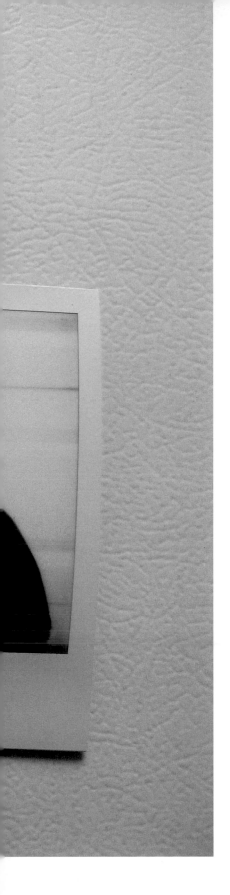

DWAYNE LUTCHNA

DWAYNE LUTCHNA
USA

#72

PX 600 SILVER
SHADE UV+ GREY
FRAME

CAMERA:
SPIRIT 600 CL

THE NAUGHTY INDEX
What happens when you ask perfectly reasonable strangers to take their clothes off in public? The Naughty Index is my attempt to interrogate the locals of my hometown – "Manchester, England, England" – destroy a few myths and undress the city ... with a cheeky smile and a Polaroid camera in hand.

Ikem Nzeribe

**IKEM NZERIBE
ENGLAND**

**PX 600 SILVER
SHADE**   **#73**

**CAMERA:
SLR 680**

JUST LIKE A COMIC

The genesis of this project is based on just two things: 1. The PX 680 FF film, which was great for doing delicate pastel-colored emulsion lifts. 2. I'm your classic comic-jerk guy, and like to draw on instant films. Put these things together, add a bit of humor and ... voilà!

B - kini.

**PAOLO MORI
ITALY**

**PX 680 COLOR
SHADE**

#74

**CAMERA:
SX 70 POLASONIC
MODEL 2
WITH ND FILTER**

IMPOSSIBLE CUPS
Turn your coffee mug into a work of art!
Use emulsion lifts to jazz up boring
dishes! Did you forget a birthday or an-
niversary? Now you'll always have
back-up gifts in your cupboard as long
as you have some Impossible photos
to throw on them.

Katie Sykes (signature)

KATIE SYKES
USA

PX 680 COLOR
SHADE

CAMERA:
ONE 600

#75

CE N'EST PAS
UN CHAPEAU.

IMPOSSIBLE EMBOSSER
Given my passion for material effects,
I decided to couple instant photography
with metal. This allows you to expand
your photo with a message and achieve
an exceptional result.

[signature]

**ALAN MARCHESELLI
ITALY**   #76

**PX 600 SILVER
SHADE GOLD FRAME**

**CAMERA:
ONE 600**

IMPOSSIBLE (MESSAGE) IN A BOTTLE
Give a message to people you care about
in a romantic way, and have some emulsion lift fun at the same time: Send an
Impossible photo in a bottle.

Carmen Palermo

**CARMEN PALERMO
ITALY**

**PX 100 SILVER
SHADE**

**CAMERA:
SX 70 SONAR**

#77

MUSIC BOXES

This project is the fruit of combining two of my greatest passions: music and instant photography. When I was asked to show some of my photographic work, I had the idea to add sounds and loops to scenes I had captured on instant film. The soundtrack to these photos can be heard through headphones.

Daniel González Fuster

DANIEL GONZÁLEZ FUSTER
SPAIN

PX 100 SILVER SHADE

PX 680 COLOR SHADE

CAMERAS: SX 70 SLR 680

#78

OPTICAL ILLUSION
I'm not a magician but I still like optical illusions. And I like playing with miniaturized objects or scenes to create unusual optical effects in my analog instant photos.

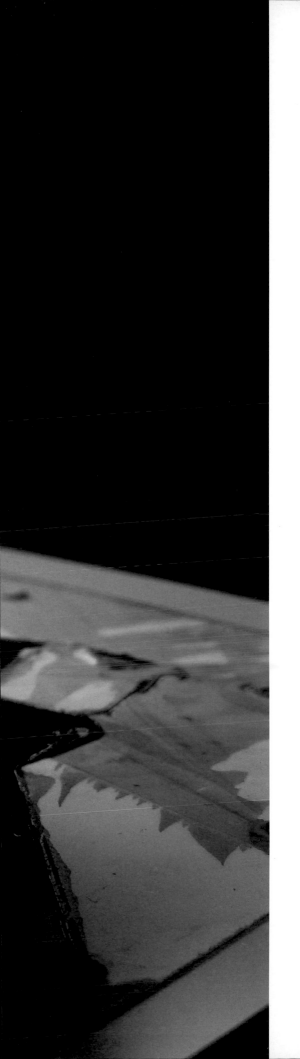

C. Woywood

CARSTEN WOYWOOD
GERMANY

PZ 680 COLOR   #79
SHADE

CAMERA:
POLAROID MACRO 5
SLR CAMERA

IMPOSSIBLE TO FORGET WALL
We really love taking Impossible photos
of what we call "Polaroid moments,"
for example when we are on a trip or at
a gathering with dear friends. We use
this wall to remember those precious
moments and be grateful for them.

**ALFREDO PRADO
AUSTRALIA**

**PX 70 COLOR
SHADE**

**CAMERA:
SX 70 1000**

#80

CONTRACT FORMATION
You hate legal contracts that take 1001 pages to describe something simple? Contracts are a bit like mushrooms. Yes, some may kill you. But others make you happy and it's a gorgeous thing to document contract closure with instant photos – surely any legal expert will confirm contract law conformity.

WOLFY

Wolle van der Lohn

**WOLLE VAN
DER LOHN
SWITZERLAND**

**PZ 600 SILVER
SHADE**

**CAMERA:
IMAGE/SPECTRA**

#81

STAND UP

We were looking for an unusual way
to share some of our favorite Impossible
photos. After making various clay
models, we ended up with this design,
called a Stand Up, but nicknamed Look.
By now the family consists of copper,
bronze and chrome Stand Ups.
Have a Look!

Joost Verburg
&
Karen Glandrup

JOOST VERBURG & KAREN GLANDRUP NETHERLANDS

PX 600 SILVER SHADE GOLD FRAME

PX 600 SILVER SHADE BLACK FRAME

CAMERA: ONE 600

#82

LIGHT IT UP AND BURN IT DOWN

Want to enjoy the darker months with
the light and romance of a candle,
but afraid of real fire? Light up and burn
down an Impossible Candle!

Barbara

BARBARA WERTH
NETHERLANDS

PX 600 SILVER SHADE

CAMERA: SX 70 WITH FILTER

#83

INSTANT ORGANIZER
We all have photos that turn out to be duds. Instead of throwing them away, use them to keep other instant film projects organized!

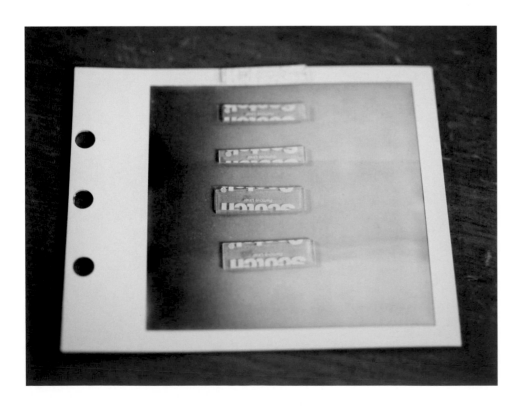

Kimberlee Oberski (signature)

KIMBERLEE OBERSKI
USA

PX 70 COLOR
SHADE

PX 600 SILVER
SHADE

CAMERAS:
SX 70
600

#84

IMPOSSIBLE MANIPULATION

Looking for a way to alienate my Impossible photos, I was delighted to find out that classic photo manipulation was applicable not only to Polaroid film but also to Impossible film. Generally I'm not a fan of manipulation, but I can't stop with this one and its truly amazing results.

REMO CAMEROTA
USA

PX 70 COLOR
SHADE PUSH!

#85

CAMERAS:
SX 70 FOLDING

IF YOU JUMP, I JUMP

Tired of posed pictures of your friends?
Next time tell them to jump and you'll
be surprised how much fun they'll have
and who'll jump the highest.

Claudia Meng

**CLAUDIA & FRIENDS
AUSTRIA**

**PX 600 SILVER
SHADE**

**CAMERAS:
SLR 680
600**

#86

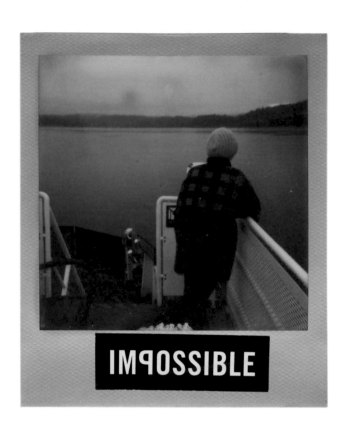

IMPOSSIBLE CHAIN LETTER

This international project connects inspired people, unique photos and wild stories, without the need for the World Wide Web. Based on the concept of a chain letter, everyone involved adds a photo and a new part of the story, creating a manifold analog narrative result.

Telling a Short Story with „9" Impossible Instant Images

1.) He who dwells in the heart of all analog instant image enthusiasts, he who destroyed their fear to lose this unique medium, he who taught Polaroid not to give up – NEVER – he who is our most respected Mr. Florian Kaps! To him i give my salutations. He makes us happy he makes us smile in summer and in winter time...

ave heidelberger

2. Being second in line, I needed some time, to come up with a rhyme that would mach the word "time"... Merry Christmas to all instant photography lovers! Peace, love and understanding! :)

IGNAS KUTAVICIUS

③ For exploration to space they appointed Dr.Florian, surrounded by mystery and guarded by festive gas masks. For memories were made to be remembered, documented, lost in boxes, forgotten in albums. ready to be awoken, I wait... Through winter cheers and summer smiles... salutations star boy, i won't tell them i caught you sleeping. Dr Floian will be here soon my analog companions. For the world must learn of his Name, Learn that nothing is impossible...

BEN INNOCENT.

IV

9lacing a hand on the cold salted rail sends tingling nerves into spasm. A mist-shrouded shore, escapes clarity found only in nature. Moments to breathe the air of ancestors, taken in context. An image of emulsion, shuttered not in silence. Placing all dreams in the **IM9OSSIBLE**.

GORD IVERSEN

5 As the ship approaches the shore, the ancestors await. They pay respect to the impossible journey with flowers and beads and visions of a world full of magical instants yet to be captured.

DAVE BIAS

please continue on the 2. page

Ave Heidelberger

AVE HEIDELBERGER
AUSTRIA

PX 70 COLOR
SHADE

PX 600 SILVER
SHADE

PX 680 COLOR
SHADE

CAMERA:
SX 70
600

#87

COASTERS

When you have guests coming over, place their drinks on the most unusual coaster ever – an Impossible photo. This not only looks fantastic, it also provides a conversation topic you're passionate about. To protect your beloved photos, simply laminate them with a transparent plastic cover.

Weronika Gajda (signature)

**WERONIKA GAJDA
FRANCE**

**PX 100 SILVER
SHADE**

**PX 600 SILVER
SHADE**

**PX 680 COLOR
SHADE**

#88

**CAMERAS:
SX 70
600**

IT'S MONDRIAN TIME

The idea is to bring color contrasts into black and white photos in an unusual manner: by using colored screens, you remain in an analog working style, while obtaining technical results that can't be achieved with any computer program.

ALAN MARCHESELLI
ITALY

PZ 600 SILVER
SHADE

#89

CAMERA:
IMAGE/SPECTRA

HOUSE OF CARDS

Wanting to take my photos out of the box and bring them to life, I created the House of Cards – inspired by the architecture of New York, which I love to photograph. This project was composed of photos of the Flatiron Building, one of my favorites in the city.

Josie Keefe

**JOSIE KEEFE
USA**

**PX 70 COLOR
SHADE**

**CAMERA:
SX 70**

#90

HOW HIGH CAN YOU GO?

The Himalayan sun is rising. The prayer flags are blowing in the sharp wind, sending "Om Mani Padme Hum" in all directions. Encircled by great pinnacles of ice, we struggle to breathe the fresh air – it's freezing. High above the Himalayan clouds, we have made it to our "Everest" at 5,416 meters. How high can you go with your Polaroid camera?

Guillaume

**GUILLAUME POLLINO
AUSTRALIA**

**PX 680 COLOR
SHADE**

**CAMERA:
600**

#91

IMPOSSIBLE FLIPBOOK
One rainy evening I thought, Why not
stay at home and create a good old flipbook instead of going to the cinema?
There I was, turning Impossible photos
into a little stop-motion movie.

DANIEL DÖRING
GERMANY

PX 70 COLOR
SHADE FF

AMERA:
X 70

#92

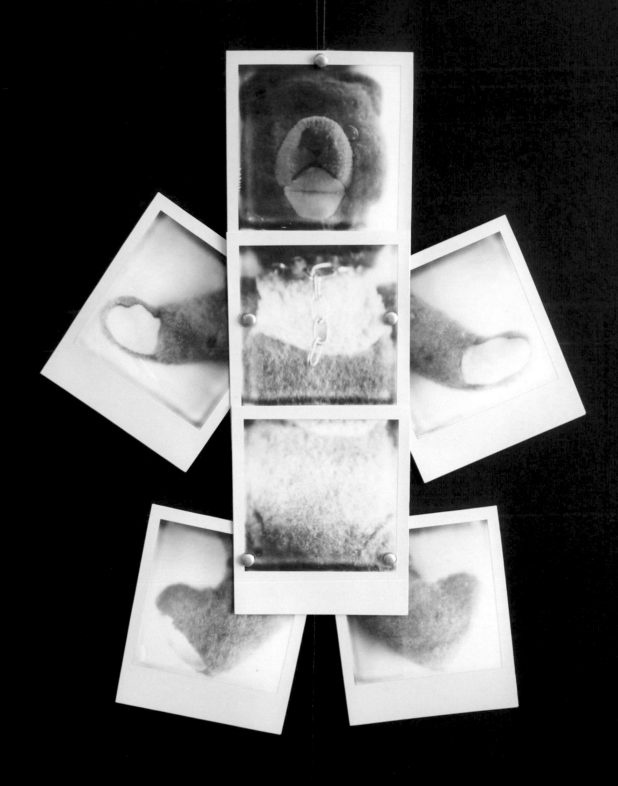

JUMPING NICKY
Jumping jacks are a traditional toy in
almost every country, made from wood,
paper or any material you can imagine.
So they seem to lend themselves well to
being made from Impossible photos.

Barbara

**BARBARA WERTH
NETHERLANDS**

**PX 600 SILVER
SHADE**

**CAMERA:
SX 70
WITH ND FILTER**

#93

IMPOSSIBLE ADVENT CALENDAR
Celebrate the beautiful days of Advent
and the anticipation of Christmas by
creating an amazing Impossible Advent
Calendar with your favorite memories
captured in Impossible photos through-
out the year.

Ulrike Kobler (signature)

**ULRIKE KOBLER
AUSTRIA**

**PX 680 COLOR
SHADE**

**CAMERA:
SX 70
WITH ND FILTER**

#94

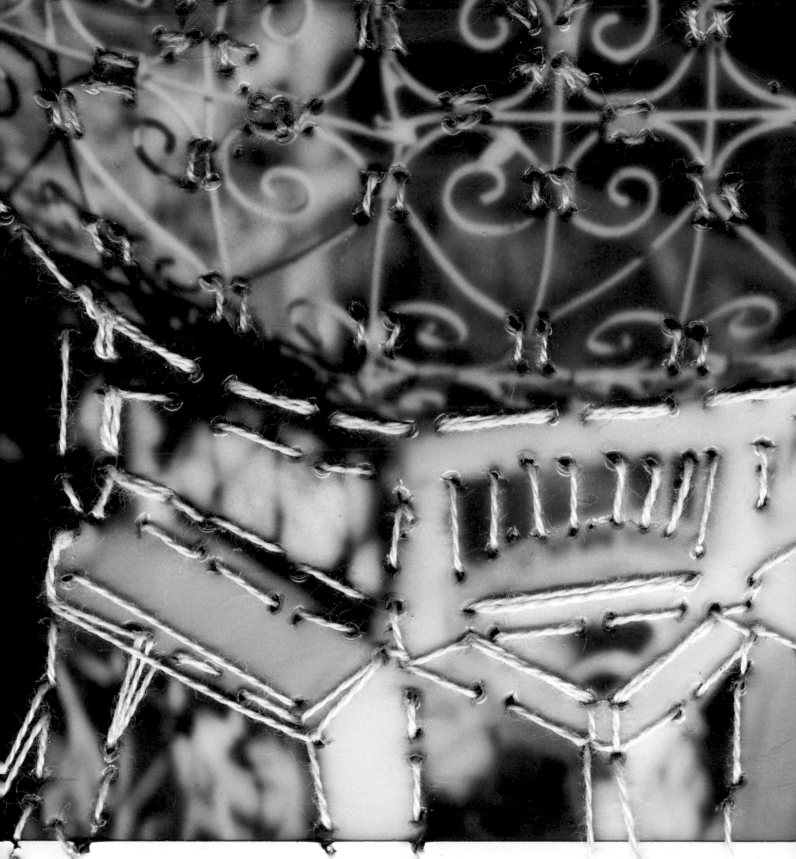

STITCHES

Sew Impossible photos together, connecting them in multiple conceptually interesting ways – for narrations, mosaics and more. You can also sew additional embroidery onto their surface or simply stitch patterns onto them with yarn and thread.

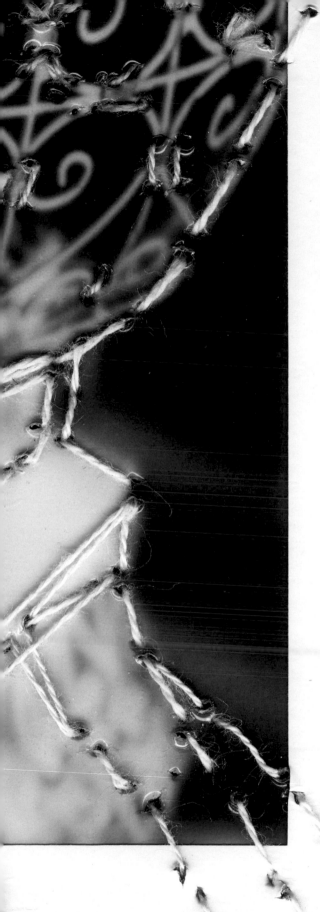

Lia Sáile

**LIA SÁILE
AUSTRIA**

**PX 70 SILVER
SHADE**

**CAMERA:
SX 70 ALPHA A1**

#95

CREATIVE WRITING

On our daily trips through the city
we pass by many different signs, letters
and numbers. As our attention is always busy with thoughts and dreams,
most of the time we don't notice them.
My project makes me stop thinking,
opens my eyes and allows me to see all
the beautiful possibilities.

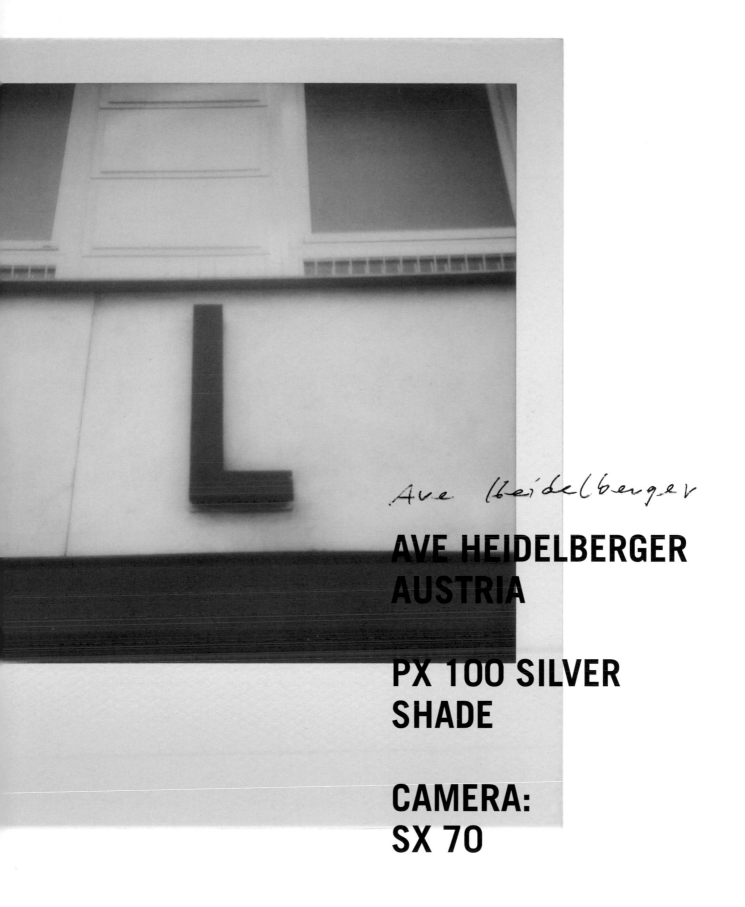

Ave Heidelberger

**AVE HEIDELBERGER
AUSTRIA**

**PX 100 SILVER
SHADE**

**CAMERA:
SX 70**

#96

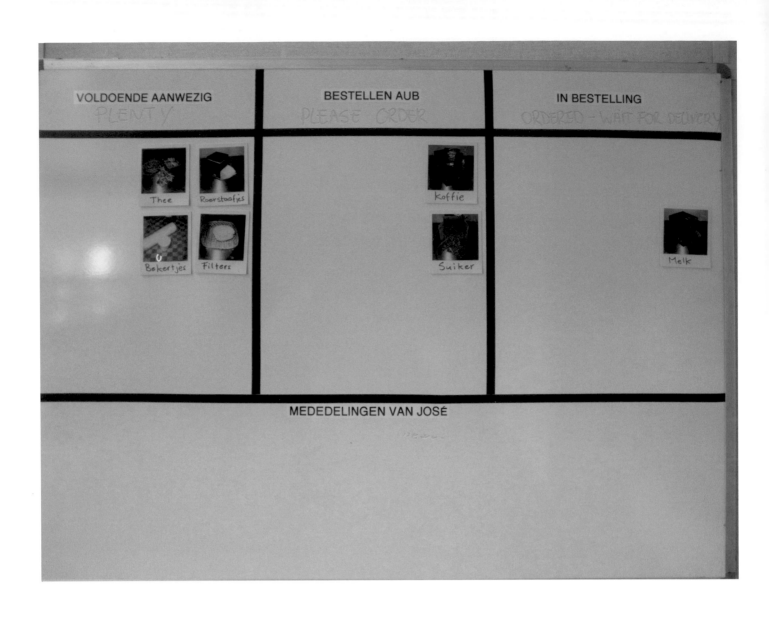

KITCHEN SUPPLY CHAIN MANAGEMENT

At the Impossible Factory in Enschede, we spend our lunch breaks in what used to be the huge old Polaroid restaurant. Here we find coffee, tea, sugar and other nutritious delights. To see what we still have in stock and know when we're running out of things, we created this chart for a quick and catchy overview.

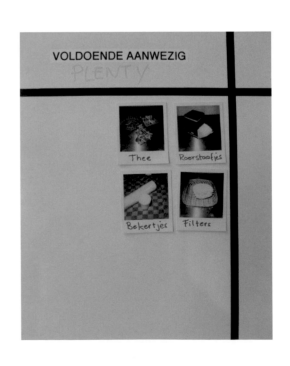

IM9OSSIBLE
Factory Team

**IMPOSSIBLE
FACTORY TEAM
NETHERLANDS**

**PX 680 COLOR
SHADE**

**CAMERA:
ONE 600**

#97

SX 70 LONG EXPOSURE
I love the quiet of the night and how you
can hear time slowly passing by.
By taking long-exposure shots using a
Polaroid SX 70 or 680 camera, I manage
to capture these serene moments with
their constant silent movement.

Jimmy Lam

JIMMY LAM
HONGKONG

PX 70 COLOR
SHADE

CAMERA:
SX 70

#98

BIRTHDAY CARDS

I always like giving something special
to a special birthday child. For really
unique birthday cards, I like putting two
or more photos together to create one
picture with a cinematic super-wide feeling. Sometimes the photos don't line
up exactly, but that only adds dynamics
and suspense.

**RAUL DIAZ
FRANCE**

**PX 680 COLOR
SHADE**

**CAMERA:
SLR 680**

#99

DAISY CHAIN

Adorn yourself in your favorite
blooms that will never wither.

Rosanna Barson

**ROSANNA BARSON
AUSTRALIA**

**PX 680 COLOR
SHADE**

**CAMERA:
SLR 680**

#100

PICTURE IN PICTURE
This technique was first practiced with a famous webmaster in London. Attention – highly addictive, as this is much more effective, faster and cheaper than undergoing plastic surgery. A fun project that no digital camera can keep pace with and one that made me fall in love with analog photography.

**FLORIAN KAPS
AUSTRIA**

**PX 600 SILVER
SHADE**

**CAMERA:
SLR 680 WITH
MACRO LENS**

#101

TURN YOUR HEAD

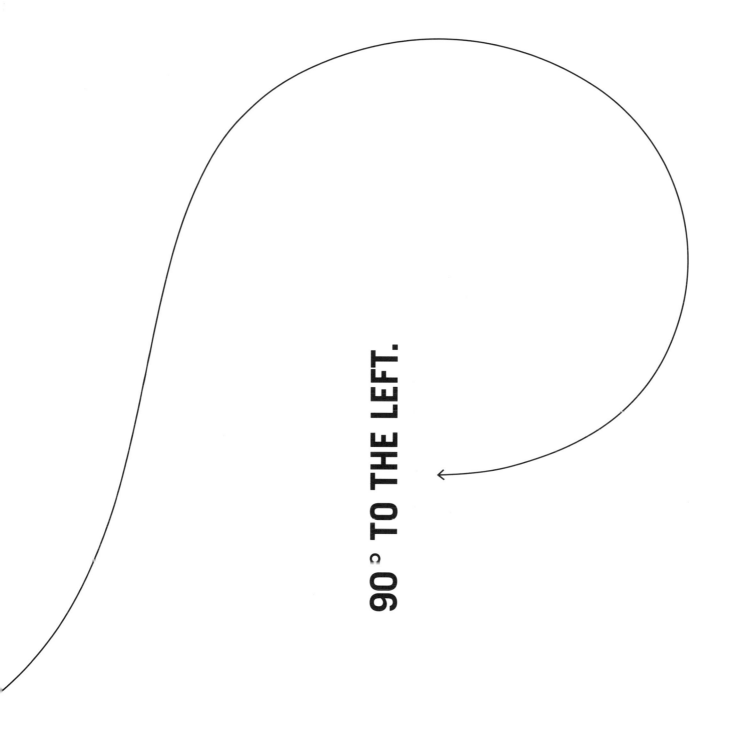

90° TO THE LEFT.

#1 Step 1: Put your camera on a tripod and focus.

CLAREESE HILL
LIGHT SCRIBBLES

Set up about 1.5–3 m (6–10 ft) from the camera with a penlight. The further away, the smaller the splash of light.

Step 3: Release the shutter and make scribble motions with the light.

Step 4: You'll have about 1–3 minutes.

Step 5: To create depth, turn off the light, spin the focusing knob, then scribble more.

Step 6: Switch from focused to unfocused to experiment with the depth you achieve.

Step 7: Scribble until the shutter closes and the photo is ejected. Enjoy your result and learn from it.

#2 Step 1: Use the template to print out a transparency to

LAWRENCE CHAM
DESIGN YOUR OWN FILTER

By printing a pattern onto a transparency you transform any Impossible Spectra cameras.

Step 2: Design your own unique template. Download a sample at: http://www.thirtysix.com.sg/main/?p=4069

Step 3: Print and cut out your transparency.

Step 4: Place the transparency in the cartridge, making sure it's on top of the black slide.

Step 5: Insert the cartridge and you're ready to shoot.

#3 Step 1: Take a photo.

JONATHAN THOMAS
NUDE STUDIES

Step 2: Check using a ballpoint pen.

Step 3: Cut open the film and pull it apart from the back.

Step 4: Soak the two pieces in water.

Step 5: Optional: Scrub/scratch the film with anything abrasive.

Step 6: Float in water and scan.

Step 7: Adjust color, curves, inverse, etc.

Step 8: Print.

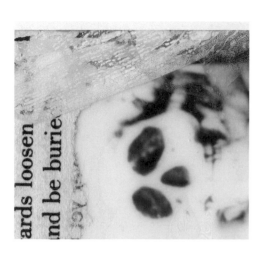

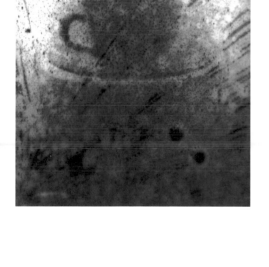

ards loosen
nd be burie

#4: Take a film slide from the box by cracking the box

MAX SCHNEIDER
POLAROID PAINTINGS

Step 1: ...fishing a single slide out of the box. (No camera is used in this process.)

Step 2: ...ambient light situations. You may want to experiment with different levels or colors of ambient light.

Step 3: Work the chemicals manually over the photo from the bottom up. You can use different stencils and objects to achieve a variety of patterns and forms.

Step 4: Experiment.

#5: Take a photo – the fresher the photo, the clearer

ELIN JONES
IMPOSSIBLE PHOTOGRAMS

Step 1: ...ency will be.

Step 2: Cut along all sides.

Step 4: Carefully peel apart the layers.

Step 5: Go to a darkroom.

Step 6: Put the Polaroid transparency directly onto photographic paper – under a glass contact frame is best.

Step 7: Make a test strip to decide on exposure and contrast.

Step 8: Make a final print.

#6: You need two photos: a portrait, and a ruined one.

MARION PLANCIAUX
CHEMICAL SOULS

Step 1: ...by cutting the edge and removing the back. Keep the transparent part

Step 2: ...start playing with the chemical substance using a wet sponge and some cotton balls to create movement.

Step 3: Let it dry for an hour, then stick it to the remaining portrait photo.

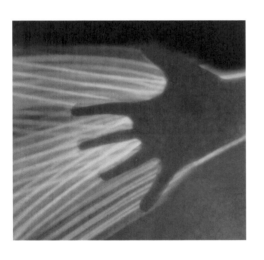

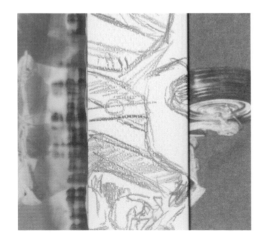

#7

Step 1: Take a printed postcard, poster, tray, etc.

GIAN GUIDO ZURLI
READY MADE

Step 2: ...photograph the image/Spectra camera with a Close-Up Stand Duplicator over the object/part you want to duplicate.

Step 3: Take your shot.

Step 4: Let the photo develop and use clay-modeling tools to begin the manipulation.

Step 5: Frame the photo by moving around the chemicals inside using a blunt tool.

Step 6: Flip the photo to add more manipulations – be creative!

Step 7: Attach the photo to the original object, aligning the main features.

#8

Step 1: Set the camera on a tripod.

FERNANDA MONTORO
HEAVENLY CREATURES

Step 2: ...position yourself behind your model.

Step 3: Turn off all lights.

Step 5: With your flashlight, illuminate her/him with rapid upward movements, contouring the whole silhouette.

Step 6: Repeat as many times as possible before the camera ejects the photo. Tip: The SX70 camera's long exposure feature should give you enough time. If you need more time and control, open the camera's front compartment (where you load film) after pressing the shutter. Do your light painting. Then close the compartment, press the shutter and the camera will eject the photo.

#9

Step 1: Choose a simple background for your subject.

RAUL DIAZ
SUPER WIDE

Step 2: ...object in front of the background and look through your camera. Now, what you are ...to divide the subject into two separate photos.

Step 3: Try to find something that will overlap and won't change from photo to photo, e.g. an extended arm, hair, clothing – anything that will join the two photos as one once put together. Note: This works best with SLR cameras (SX70, 680, etc.)

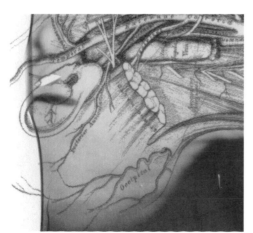

#10 Find an interesting anatomy diagram and scan it.

MARTIN CARTWRIGHT
GRAY'S ANATOMY

Step 1: ... develop and wait for it to

Print a copy of the diagram roughly 15% larger than the photo.

Step 4: Cut the film's edges and peel the two sides apart to create a transparency.

Step 5: Soak in warm water, gently brushing off any white residue.

Step 6: Transfer the emulsion to the printed scan.

Step 7: Stretch and distort it to fit as closely as possible.

Step 8: Tape to a board to dry flat.

#11 Heat your oven to 100 °C / 212 °F.

EUGEN NOUJAEV
BAKING IMPOSSIBLE

Step 3: Push the baking sheet into the oven.

... photos or a baking sheet.

Step 5: Take them out as soon as they reached the desired level of deformation.

Step 6: Let the baked Impossible photos cool.

Step 7: Carefully peel your shots from the white frame and any other undesired remains.

#12 Prepare A5-size pieces of card stock.

FRANTICHAM
DIARY FROM AN IMPOSSIBLE LOVE STORY

... possible photograph documenting your day

Make a today using anything...

Step 4: Add address and stamp and send it to your loved one.

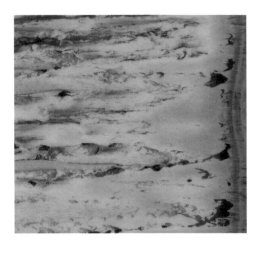

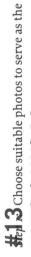

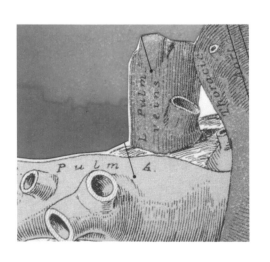

#13 Choose suitable photos to serve as the

EVER DUNDAS
GREETING CARDS

Step 2: Glue your collage pieces onto them.

Step 3: ...reeting on the bottom of the photo/collage or, as I have done, write on the back of the card.

#14 Take a roll of duct tape and lay out 6 strips 8"

EVAN M. CERDA
IMPOSSIBLE DUCT TAPE
DECORATION

...connected to each other.

Step 2: Repeat step 1 but lay the tape strips face down... strips face up.

Step 3: ...a duct tape.

Step 4: Fold in half hamburger style.

Step 5: Tape the side of the fold and repeat step 3.

Step 6: Fold the wallet into three sections.

Step 7: Add four credit card spaces by repeating steps 1 and 2, but change the sizing to 3"x4".

#15 Expose your failed photos to heat to make them

MELANIE J. ALEXANDROU
GROW YOUR OWN
POLAROID (BOOK)

Step 2: Cut out and fold cardboard into an accordion-... in shorter pieces of card

Step 3: Attach one photo to each page of the accordion book.

Step 4: Apply Letraset letter transfers to each photo in order of its size.

MILK.

#16
Take Impossible photos of everyday tasks or it milk to buy, bills to pay, etc.

BEN INNOCENT
IMPOSSIBLE REMINDER

Step 2: Label / decorate them.

Step 3: ...the Polaroid title frame reading "Things to remember!"

Step 4: Using Blu-Tack or Impossible magnetic wall stars, stick the photos in a visible place, e.g. on cupboards, the fridge, the front door.

Step 5: Remember the previously forgotten.

#17
Take an Impossible shot.

ROXANNE DANER
GOUACHE + POLAROID

Step 2: ...water and a paintbrush.

Step 3: Mix the gouache with a little bit of water so that

Step 4: Paint on the photo.

Step 5: Apply a second coat after the paint dries to ensure a solid illustration.

#18
Take a photo and carefully cut off the frame.

ALAN MARCHESELLI
IMPOSSIBLE HIGH THICKNESS PHOTOS

...base of about 2 mm of transparent resin (found at any art supply shop).

...fill...with 4 – 5 mm resin (0,2").

...the photo with

Step 5: Dip a toothpick into solvent-based glass paint.

Step 6: Use the toothpick to draw in the resin, mixing your favorite colors.

Step 7: Wait 24 hours, then you can detach the picture from the silicon mold.

Step 8: The resin will still be soft and you can cut it along the borders of your picture.

Step 9: Wait 12 hours and enjoy.

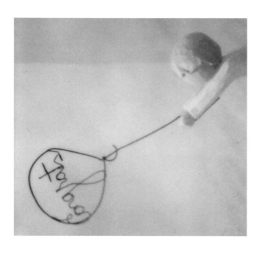

#19 Cut off the white frame.

ANDREW KUA
UNMASKING NEGATIVITY

Step 1: ... water, gently peel off the top transparent layer. With the remaining emulsion,

Step 3: Under a running tap, gently rub off the white substance on the negative.

Step 4: Pour bleach on the negative and under the running tap quickly (and gently) rub off the brown layer.

Step 5: Repeat step 4 with diluted bleach if necessary, until desired results appear.

Step 6: Let dry. Video tutorial at: http://www.fuzzyeyeballs.com/blog/?p=4960

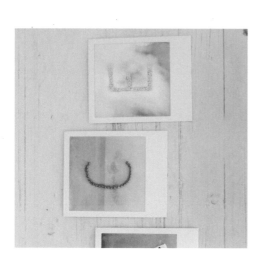

#20 Know that there is no such thing as a wasted

CÉCILE DE VRIES
2012

Step 2: Collect lots of scrapbook material.

Step 3: Feel the urge to spread a message.

Step 4: Use your imagination.

Step 5: Get that creativity out of the box!

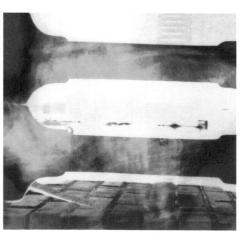
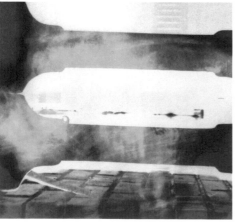

#21 Take an Impossible ND pack filter.

BEN INNOCENT
IMPOSSIBLE APOSTLE

Step 1: ... you want to spread on it.

Step 3: Place the filter on a film pack and take the photo. ... clear, or it may be obscured when exposed.

Step 4: Write anything else you like on the back of the photo.

Step 5: Share the message, be it by giving away, offering to take a picture for a stranger to keep or allowing someone to find the mysterious picture by a natural crossing of paths.

#24 Look at your old Lego figures, then set them up as they were in a film studio.

ENRICO FRENI

Step 1:

Add impossible photos to the scenery to recreate

INVADING LEGO WORLD WITH IMPOSSIBLES

Step 2:

#23 Create a transparency: Take a high-contrast photo,

BRITTA HERSHMAN

Step 1: film, of a simple subject that will work well as a negative. Remove

IMPOSSIBLE SUN PRINT

using a hair dryer and peel apart carefully. Let the transparency dry.

Step 2: Place directly on an unexposed sheet of sun print paper. Use Plexiglas or glass to keep it flat.

Step 3: Expose outdoors in direct sunlight, until the visible parts of the blue paper become faded. This should only take a few minutes.

Step 4: Remove the glass and transparency. Dip your paper in a dish of cold water and watch it develop in just a few seconds. Your final photo will be a blue and white negative of the original.

#22 Take any Impossible photo you like; I prefer

BERND P. OEHMEN

Step 1:

Step 2: Arrange different objects on your scanner.

PX FILM AND MY SCANNER

Step 3: Add me when

Step 4: Scan the result and enjoy it.

#25 Sort through your photos and collect any prints

CANDICE MORATO
IMPOSSIBLE BOOKPLATES

Step 1: ...form into bookplates.

Step 2: Scribble your message and name onto the photo

Step 3: Stick the photo to the inside cover of a book using double-sided tape.

Step 4: Now you're ready to share your books with your friends, and you have a personal record of ownership for anyone who may inherit your books in the future.

#26 Take a photo.

ELIZA ACOSTA
TYPEWRITER

Step 1: ...ack the photo into a mechanical typewriter.

Step 2: ...sertion of words onto the white border. This works best one word at a time. You may need to rearrange or hold the photo to keep it straight.

Step 4: If you need to, erase words by licking your finger and wiping them away.

#27 Take two people – preferably a fine-looking

ERIC SOSSO
IMPOSSIBLE LOVE

Step 1: couple.

Step 2: Take a photo while they're kissing. Be careful: ...fter the kiss is real, so don't hassle them during the kiss, just shoot.

Step 3: Let the photo fully develop.

Step 4: Use a stapler to connect their mouths in the photo.

Step 5: Whatever happens now, they will be kissing forever in this beautiful, unforgettable Impossible photo.

#28
Step 1 Take interesting photos.

FERDINAND VYKOUKAL
TRANSFER ONTO AN OBJECT

... the ... lift procedure but leave the emulsion on the transparent front ...

Step 3: Place the plastic with the emulsion in the desired position on the object, e.g. on a Styrofoam ball.

Step 4: Now carefully begin to transfer the emulsion to your object from the corner to the center of the emulsion.

Step 5: Let it dry and varnish it. Take a photo of your final object.

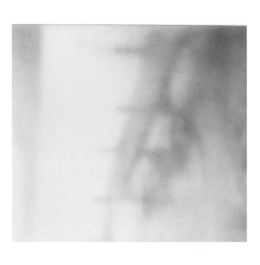

#29
Step 1 Find some models and have them lean against a

GABRIELE PAGANI
DESTRUCTURE

Step 2: Grab a Polaroid camera capable of macro work. ... system with a macro attachment, but any camera that can close-focus could be used

Step 3: Take some close-up pictures of body details. I used the face, the hand, the foot and the belly, but the choices are almost endless.

Step 4: Mount the photos together. I used a square shape, but vertical or horizontal compositions are also interesting.

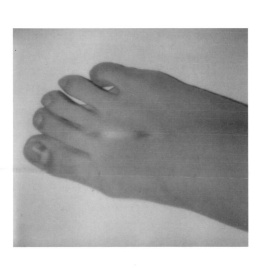

#30
Step 1 Get pieces of clear textured glass (5 – 6 square ... glass supply store. Look through them first to make sure you like the ... colored pieces work too, but

GENEVIEVE NEAL
ALTERED VISIONS

... compensate for this loss of light with the lighten/darken button on your camera.

Step 2: Place the glass in front of your lens and look through the viewfinder. Move the glass around until you like how the altered view looks. Avoid blocking the flash, as it will bounce off the glass and ruin your picture.

Step 3: Once you're pleased with the effect, take the shot, develop and enjoy the new and altered view of your subject!

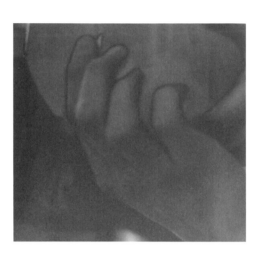

#31 *Step 1:* Save two empty film cartridges.

IGNAS KUTAVICIUS
HALF COLOR, HALF MONO CHROME

Step 2: Save two possible films, e.g. PX 600 Silver Shade and PX 680 Color Shade.

Step 3: Load images with a set of film at a time, alternating types. Don't forget to put the dark slide on top once full (8 sheets).

Step 4: Now you have cartridges that shoot different film each time you press the shutter. Place your camera on a stable surface and take two identical photos, one in color and one in black and white.

Step 5: After they develop, slice both in half.

Step 6: Now switch the two parts and tape together for two photos that are half color, half monochrome.

#32 *Step 1:* Take a photo.

INA ECHTERNACH
THE IMPOSSIBLE LAMP

Step 2: onto a sandwich bag.

Step 3: Place a tea light (in a candle holder) in the sandwich bag.

Step 4: Light the candle.

Step 5: Enjoy your new lamp.

#33 *Step 1:* Take a PX 100 Silver Shade photo with clear,

JAMES MATTHEW CARROLL
IMPOSSIBLE HEAT

Step 2: Shield from light and place face down.

Step 3: blacken layer blasts. After 30–60 seconds, see if the photo is growing visible.

Step 4: Cover light areas and give dark areas some more blasts. Pause between heating to make sure it isn't shifting too far toward orange. When the dark areas have an orange tint, allow to finish developing.

Step 5: Check the result: Not very orange? You haven't heated it enough! Everything is orange? You heated it too much!

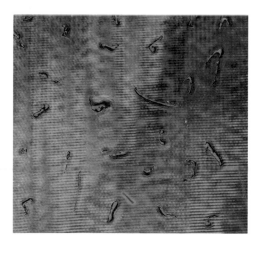

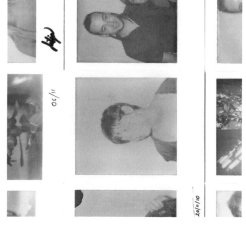

#34 Step 1: Take photos of your family and friends, as well as

JOSEAN MOLINA GIL
ME, MYSELF AND I

Step 2: Write a memory on the white frame or have it signed by your loved ones.

Step 3: Assemble all the photos on a wall or any other place you look at often, and enjoy these preserved moments with the people who make your world.

#35 Step 1: Shoot any type of Impossible instant film.

JONATHAN CAMPOLO
MYSTERY MANIPULATION

Step 2: Using the normal process as normal.

Step 3: Using a flat surface to add friction with a coin, paper clip or chisel, apply pressure to the back (black side) of the photo.

Step 4: Allow 3 – 6 minutes for the photo to process, depending on temperature and film type.

Step 5: Flip over your photo to reveal your exposure and mystery manipulation!

#36 Step 1: Take Impossible photos.

CHIHARU HOSHIDA
WEAR AN IMPOSSIBLE DRESS

Step 2: Transfer the emulsion onto a fabric of your choice.

Step 3: Using the emulsion adhesive add some glue.

Step 4: Wear your Impossible dress.

#37 Choose a patient model.

JONAS IKUFAVICIUS ...one position until you are done.

MULTI-SHOT PORTRAIT
...shots of face, body and background.

Step 4: When all the photos have developed, put them together and see if you have an image that satisfies you. If something isn't right, take a new shot of the part in question.

Step 5: When you feel you have all the parts you need, cut the bottom of every photo and remove the frame paper.

Step 6: Piece the image together like a puzzle.

#38 Look for addresses. The best ones are usually near ...jects or older parts of town.

KATIE SYKES

Step 2: Compose your shot wisely, because you'll be ...

ADDRESSES ARE COOL
...format.

Step 3: Paint the back of a piece of Plexiglas white with acrylic paint (2 – 3 coats). Let it dry.

Step 4: Using acid-free double-sided tape, adhere your photos to the front of the Plexiglas in a grid of 5 rows and 5 photos per row.

Step 5: (Optional.) Drill a hole 1 inch from the top center of the piece. Hang on the wall with a nail.

Step 6: (Important.) Bask in the glory you just created.

#39 Organize your books by genre.

LENA BURGGRAF with motifs matching the different genres.

ARRANGING BOOKS IN AN IMPOSSIBLE WAY
...corresponding genre. ...shelf, marking the order of your books.

#40 Open your Image System camera.

FRANK BROUWER
access the controls on the back.

DOUBLE EXPOSURE

Using the film twice (or more), I always put the exposure control to the darker setting. (Slide the button down next to the black arrow.)

Step 4: Focus and take a photo, but DON'T release the button.

Step 5: Close the camera while holding down the button. Once it's closed, you can let go of the button.

Step 6: Reopen the camera and take your second picture normally. The camera should now spit out your double exposure.

#41 Take photos that repeat the same characters, in different places.

FEDERICO CORPIERI

PICTURE STORY

Step 2: Add comic-style dialogue.

Step 3: and you're done.

LITTLE ACHIS'LIONS

#42 Bend a wide paperclip into a triangle.

MARIA DONATA VILLA
the back of the battery to use as a hook.

BRING YOUR IMPOSSIBLES.

EVERYWHERE
the battery. Don't try to fit more than 8 per case, as you could ruin them.

Step 5: Hang the battery wherever you like.

Step 6: Enjoy your photos.

Step 7: There are a thousand ways to customize this project: Slip Christmas lights under the photos, or hang them on a wire coat hanger as a mini exhibit.

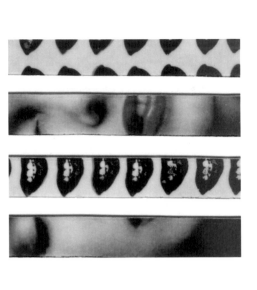

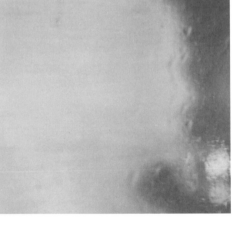

#43 Grow your garden with love, watch special flowers

MARIANNA BATTOCCHIO

MY IMPOSSIBLE HERBARIUM

Step 2: Shoot any Impossible photo.

favorite creative technique.

Step 4: Carefully open the photo and remove some of the emulsion.

Step 5: Place your favorite flower on the film and close the photo again. Make sure the photo as well as the flower have dried.

Step 6: Use a diary to collect all the photos of your favorite flowers. By adding their botanical names you can create your Impossible Herbarium.

#44 Use an old desktop calendar.

DOROTA WAGNER

IMPOSSIBLE YEAR

Step 1: ... a few centimeters around the binding. Don't just rip the pages off

Step 3: Cut the calendar's stand to fit the photo size.

Step 4: Pick your favorite Impossible photos (12 for 12 months).

Step 5: On the reverse side of the instant photos, draw / apply the name of the month and the dates. (I used alphabet stickers.)

Step 6: Attach the photos to the remaining pieces of the calendar pages with adhesive tape or glue.

#45 Take two photos.

MASSIMILIANO MUNER

(S)COMPOSITE

Step 3: Create a new composition combining the strips.

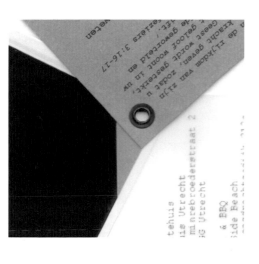

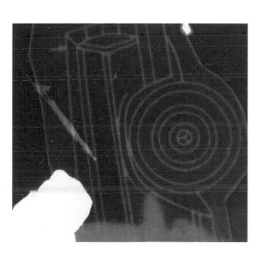

#46 Use an Image Pro Camera.

MASSIMO BATTISTA
Step 3: Shoot your photos.

A TRIBUTE TO ALFRED
Step 1: ...composed of ... bit of acrylic

HITCHCOCK

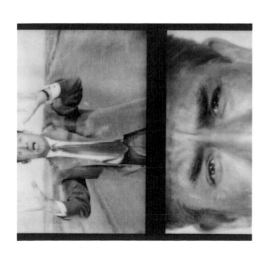

#47 Take a photo.

MICHAELA SCAGNETTI
Step 3: Cut the frame off.

DO YOU BELIEVE IN NEGATIVE?
Step 2: ...elevator and ...

Step 4: ... Battle roll with an emulsion

Step 5: Carefully peel off the emulsion and lift it onto a sheet of watercolor paper.

Step 6: Hold the remaining white side under hot running water.

Step 7: Soon you'll see a magic "negative" to preserve.

#48 Take as many gorgeous pictures of the two of you

MIRIAM VAN 'T HOVEN
Step 2: Print the day's schedule on carbon paper and cut

WEDDING INVITATIONS
Step 1: ...

Step 3: Print the invitation text on old brown cardboard and cut to photo size.

Step 4: Put all three components together with copper-colored Jersey fasteners.

Step 5: Print addresses on old brown envelopes.

Step 6: Send to your beloved friends and family!

#51 Take photos and create transparencies by

GIOVANNA CHEMI
ON-OFF-ON-OFF

Step 1: ...each photo with a hairdryer and peeling it apart. The photo should stick to the ...in space...

Step 2: With a dark slide, cut out silhouettes of drawings and letters.

Step 3: Hang the transparencies and dark slide on the lamp with metal clips.

Step 4: Turning the light on illuminates the photos and projects your writing onto the wall.

Step 5: On, off ... on, off ...

#50 First of all, don't get rid of your ruined photos.

RUDY FORCE
USER MANUAL
FOR BEGINNERS

Step 1: ...collect your...

Step 2: Find a nice photo album or an old book.

Step 3: ...attach... each page.

Step 4: ...explanation of why the photo went wrong, and what you should and shouldn't do next time.

Step 5: Share your album, especially with Impossible beginners.

#49 Take photos near an airport, where you can shoot

NUNO TUDELA
AIR MOBILE

Step 1: ...planes against the blue sky. Include some clouds in the sky in your ... Let the pictures fully develop.

Step 2: Optional Step: Apply the transparencies technique to your photos.

Step 3: Use pliers to cut wires for each level of the mobile. Use string to hang the photos on both sides of the wire. Don't forget to balance every level.

Step 4: Hang your mobile from the ceiling, a tree or anywhere else.

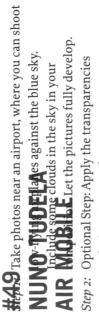

#52 Shoot pairs of Impossible photos, meaning two

SEBASTIAN OULAK

IMPOSSIBLE MEMORY

... the same frame / motif, until you ... have as many pairs as you like. (Shoot a small ... a larger number for older children.)

Step 2: Mix the photos as in a card game, turn them over and put them in rows.

Step 3: Follow the rules of the good old memory game and enjoy.

#53 Take a photo of anything that moves you.

TAYLOR SHURTE

MEMORY IN POLAROID

... inspiration to lead you to the ... materials you will need to decorate your picture. ... ors, glue, glitter, stickers, buttons, mementos or anything else you can imagine, add to your photo or around its frame.

Step 4: You end up with a framed, scrapbooked, original piece of art.

#54 Look for a nice object.

TUNG CHU

PEEL & PRESS IT

Step 3: Let the photo fully develop.

... carefully part the white frame from the black back layer.

Step 5: Slowly tear the black back layer apart.

Step 6: Push the layers back together. Use a roller for better result.

Step 7: Let the picture lie under a heavy book for 24 hours.

#55 Keep under / overexposed photos.

TOM GALLAGHER
LINE DWGS

Step 3: Use the desired tool to create a drawing.

Step 4: ... to back up using tape or glue.

Step 5: Mount or frame.

Step 6: Enjoy!

#56 Take an instant photo of a small treasure, then

SUSANNA GAUNT
HIDDEN TREASURES

the photo on a 4 x 4" board.
book to personalize it.

Step 2: Also print one out-of-focus portion of the picture

Step 3: For the book itself, find old, semi-relevant titles at used bookstores, library sales or yard sales. Glue the outside of the pages together, then cut out a compartment inside to hide the mounted photograph.

Step 4: Lastly, cover all parts of the book and photograph with encaustic wax.

#57 Take a photo of something you want to turn

Step 1

DOREEN STAHR
CREATING MY OWN REALITY

Step 2: Cut off the outermost edges of the frame.

Step 3: ... let ... for about 30 seconds. Don't let it become too hot.

Step 4: Slowly peel off the upper sheet.

Step 5: Once the transparency has cooled down, use a sharp object to scrape off the coating to create a new picture.

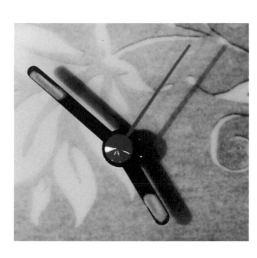

#58 Build a photo booth from cardboard boxes, glue

TOBIAS, ANNE
Step 1: together cover the surface with paper.

ASCHENBRENNER
Step 2: Hang up a curtain

AND CLAUDIA MENG
roid camera (flash

TOBIAS' PHOTO BOX
...booth.

Step 4: Cut a tiny slot for coins (optional).

Step 6: Find some props like glasses, hats, feather boas, flowers ...

Step 7: Take four pictures in a row.

Step 8: Wait until the pictures are completely developed.

Step 9: Stick the pictures together as a strip.

Step 10: Get back in the booth and have fun!

#59 Remove the battery from an empty film cassette

THOMAS HOFMAN
Step 2: Remove the holder from a car air freshener.

ON THE ROAD
Step 3: Rough the surfaces to be glued with the sand paper.

Step 4: Add epoxy on both parts (not too much) and put the parts together.

Step 5: Once the epoxy has cured completely you're "ready to go." If you transport your frame in a bag, use a dark slide to protect your Impossible photo!

#60 Use any photo you like.

CHRISTIAN DYLONG
...dle of the photo.

A UNIQUE CLOCK
Step 3: Put the clock work through it.
...umbers or anything else

to your unique, handmade clock.

#63 Take a multiple-shot portrait.

MIK BOTTIER
OBSERVER/PARTICIPANT

Step 1: ...ers of the photos using scissors.

Step 3: Divide the front positive from the negative back.

...w want a dust-free environment.

Step 5: Prepare a reflective surface.

Step 6: Compose the portrait on the surface.

Step 7: Cover with glass or plastic to keep the arrangement in place.

Step 8: Relax!

#6.2 Take an Impossible photo.

IGNAS KUTAVICIUS
ADVERTISE

...take a selection (such as website address or phone number) repeatedly in a list that will fit along the bottom side of the photo (88 mm for PX and 102 mm for PZ film photos).

Step 3: Print the list and cut it out. Make small incisions between each line of text, creating removable contact slips.

Step 4: Glue the paper to the back of your photo with the loose removable pieces hanging out.

Step 5: You can also add extra information by writing on the photo's white frame.

Step 6: Go out in the city and hang up your advertisements!

#6.1 Choose your favorite Impossible photos and

SARAH CROOKSTON
IMPOSSIBLE POP UP

...take your favorite Impossible photos and ...them. (The spine looks like a hand-folded fan and the size depends on the photo you use.)

Step 2: Write a bit about the picture on a piece of paper the same size as the photo.

Step 3: Affix the paper to the photo along the top, so it can open and close.

Step 4: Affix the photos to the spine, staggering them.

Step 5: Once the glue is dry, close the spine with the photos in it, and measure out the cover size. Affix cover.

Memo: Feliz San Valentino!
#標語: ハッピーバレンタイン
국어: 행복한 발렌타인 더

#65 Shoot a photo of the object you want to learn the foreign word for.

DEBORAH YUN photography

LEARN A LANGUAGE

Step 2: Write the new vocabulary onto the white frame.

Step 4: ... are ... regularly browse through or place the photos above your desk or in any other prominent place for effective language training.

#66 Take an overexposed PX photo.

BERND OEHMEN iPhoneography

HIGH KEY

Step 3: Add different objects to create a still life picture.

Step 4: Scan and print it out.

#64 Follow your holiday fever.

CLAUDIA MENG

VIVID POSTCARDS

Step ...: Arrive and take a photo ... stamp on it.

Step 5: Let it travel. Easy peasy.

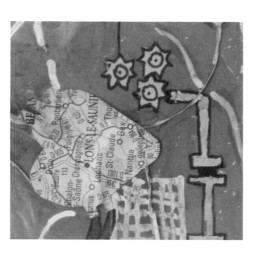

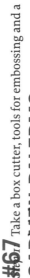
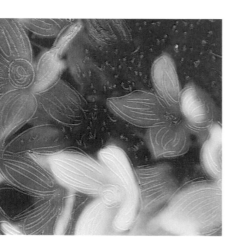

#67 Take a box cutter, tools for embossing and a

CARMEN PALERMO
Step 2: Shoot your Impossible photo and let it develop.
IMPOSSIBLE INCISION within 24 and within

72 hours.

Step 4: Incise the inner edge of the frame with a box cutter.

Step 5: Gently peel off the transparent layer from the picture.

Step 6: Use embossing tools to "draw" on the surface by applying light pressure.

Step 7: Please note that the photo will dry very quickly and you have just a minute to manipulate it.

Step 8: Dry your Impossible Incision with a hairdryer.

#68 Prepare a photo album with empty pages and

ANDREAS SCHMANSKI
Step 2: Get plenty of Impossible instant film.
WEDDING GUEST BOOK the party –
singles, couples and families.

Step 4: Attach the photos to the pages of the book.

Step 5: Collect notes and signatures from all the guests photographed.

Step 6: Be patient: Expect each person to admire the photos and read all the notes from other people before writing their own note and passing it on to the next guest to sign.

#69 Carefully cut off the edges of your photo.

HANNAH DOUCET
the glue, the transparent foil and the emulsion
INNER LIFE photo. To do so you can use a moist
tissue.

Step 3: Use different materials and techniques like drawing or collage to give a heart and inner life to your photo.

Step 4: Re-affix the transparent foil using glue or transparent tape.

Step 5: Now your photo has a heart, enjoy!

#70 Open a "Yogi Tea" teabag every morning and let

EMILIE LEFELLIC

DAILY VISUAL MEDITATION

yourself be inspired by the simplicity and depth of a great philosophical quote.

Step 1: Let the words of such wisdom curiously inspire your soul.

Step 3: Admire our world's potential to illustrate such wisdom.

Step 4: Capture it on Impossible film whenever you can.

#71 Find a model.

REMO CAMEROTA

THE GIANT TRIPTYCH IMPOSSIBLE PROJECT

Step 1: Shoot the bags without thinking.

Step 3: Scan them together as you like.

Step 4: Glue and/or bond them.

#72 Find volunteers, as many as you like.

DWAYNE LUTCHNA

REFRIGERATOR FUN

Step 1: Ask them to participate.

Step 2: Locate a simple backdrop so the focus is on the volunteer and their surroundings. I used our garage door.

Step 3: Individually, ask your volunteers to step in front of the backdrop and face left or right. Ask them to recall memories involving your other volunteer(s). Capture their expressions.

Step 4: Now, the real fun! Mix and match the photos on your fridge so they interact.

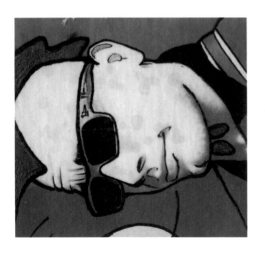

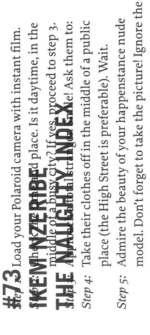

#75 Take any Impossible photo and perform an emulsion lift.

KATIE SYKES
IMPOSSIBLE CUPS

Step 2: Add a thin layer of Mod Podge to the first area of your dish before placing the emulsion.

Step 3: Gently lift up the emulsion with a soft-bristled paintbrush and place it on the dish. Dip the paintbrush in water and gently flatten out the emulsion, then use more Mod Podge to seal it on the dish. Let it dry and apply another 2 – 3 coats.

Step 4: Add as many emulsion lifts as you want. Spread them out or layer them. Note: This dish is for decorative purposes only. Have fun!

#74 Take your photo with PX 680 or any other film.

PAOLO MORI
JUST LIKE A COMIC

Step 3: Do an emulsion lift develop.

Place it on a surface of your choice. I used watercolor paper, but anything would do.

Step 5: Draw on the picture and add speech bubbles or onomatopoeia as you wish.

#73 Load your Polaroid camera with instant film.

IKE MNZERIBE
THE NAUGHTY INDEX

Find an urban setting. Is it daytime, in the middle of a busy city? If yes, proceed to step 3. Ask them to:

Step 4: Take their clothes off in the middle of a public place (the High Street is preferable). Wait.

Step 5: Admire the beauty of your happenstance nude model. Don't forget to take the picture! Ignore the amazed / shocked / excited crowd around you.

Step 6: Thank your amazing subject.

#76 Take an Impossible photo.

ALAN MARCHESELLI
IMPOSSIBLE EMBOSSER

...a flyer and separate the positive from the negative.

...emboss it using a hammer and steel stamps.

Step 4: Couple the transparent positive with the embossed metal sheet using some double-sided tape under the picture frame.

Step 5: Trim off any excess metal and enjoy your embossed Impossible photo.

#77 Choose your message and shoot it, then do an image transfer.

CARMEN PALERMO
IMPOSSIBLE (MESSAGE) IN A BOTTLE

Step 2: Carefully place the emulsion in a bottle full of water.

...the bottle and give it to the chosen friend.

Step 4: Add instructions on how he/she can perform an image transfer with the bottle's contents: Simply pour the contents into a bowl, carefully slip a carrier paper under the floating emulsion and take everything out of the water.

Step 5: The emulsion lift can be smoothed into shape with a soft brush as long as everything is still wet.

#78 Take an instant photo.

DANIEL GONZÁLEZ FUSTER
MUSIC BOXES

...the final result to an MP3 player.

Step 4: Insert the MP3 player into an empty film cartridge.

Step 5: Connect headphones.

Step 6: Press play and repeat function.

Step 7: Insert the instant photo into the film cartridge with the MP3 player.

Step 8: Seal the film cartridge with tape.

Step 9: Hold the Music Box, put the headphones on and listen to the result.

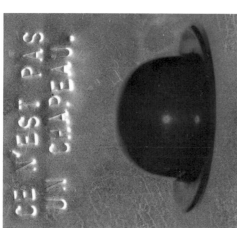

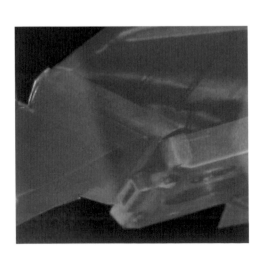

#79 Take a photo of an object or a scene of your

CARSTEN WOYWOOD
OPTICAL ILLUSION

Step 1:

Step 2: Cut out the object but don't cut it out completely to the backing layer.
Also don't cut through the back layer.

Step 3: Fold the photo, positioning and aligning it according to the perspective wanted.

Step 4: Take a photo of the folded photo using a perspective that best fits this optical effect.

Step 5: Enjoy the result.

#80 Cut 8 strings of fishing line of different lengths.

ALFREDO PRADO
IMPOSSIBLE TO FORGET WALL

Step 1:

Step 2: flatten, leaving about 11cm (4") in between. At the end of the string, tie a washer knob

Step 3: Attach the batten to the wall using removable fasteners.

Step 4: Combine the pictures, attaching them to the strings with clips.

#81 Get your transaction partner as well as the object

WOLLE VAN DER LOHN
CONTRACT FORMATION

Step 1: Polaroid camera.

Step 2: Shoot evidence possible film, one for each contract party.

Step 3: Add really important contract details on the white frame, using Impossible Photo Pens.

Step 4: This forces you to keep it short and simple.

Step 5: Et voilà – your contract closure is documented!

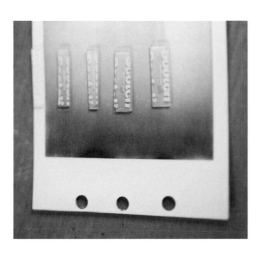

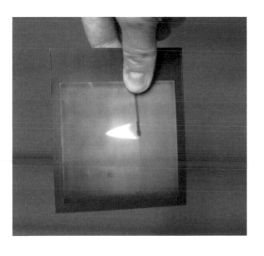

#82
The top of the "Stand Up" is split and allows you

JOOST VERBURG &
KAREN GLANDRUP
STAND UP

#83
If you're really afraid of fire, ask a friend for help.

BARBARA WERTH
LIGHT IT UP AND BURN IT
DOWN

Step 5: You can even photograph a matchbox with a burned and an unburned match.

Step 6: Build a support from Legos as high as the candle and tape the pictures to it. (You want to use your Legos again, don't you?)

Step 7: Attach the lighted candle photo. Enjoy your candle, but please … no Elton John here!

Step 8: After an hour, take out one of the middle photographs and lower the lighted top for a real burning down effect.

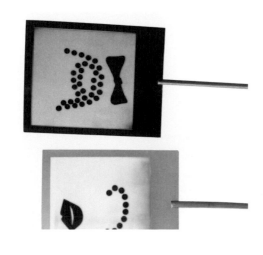

#84
Gather materials: an old daily planner or small

KIM OBERSKI
INSTANT ORGANIZER

Step 2: Punch holes in the photos to correspond with the binder's rings.

Step 3: Cover the picture area on the dud film with scrap paper, leaving the frame visible. This is the "title page" to separate / group photo projects.

Step 4: Apply double-sided tape to another dud photo, arranged so you can group 3 – 5 future photos on one dud photo.

Step 5: Place this behind a title page in your binder.

Step 6: Repeat steps 2 – 5 for as many projects as desired.

Step 7: Add tabs and labels to the title page.

#85 Gather equipment: a sharp tool (like a toothpick, ...eedle) and a hair dryer.

REMO CAMEROTA
IMPOSSIBLE MANIPULATION

Step 2: Choose your subject and take your photo.

...exposed. I use a hair dryer, but the sun may work.

Step 4: Get your sharp object and use it on the photo like a pen. Keep the photo warm to hot while pushing the emulsion around, as this also helps process the colors. Be careful not to tear the photos – unless you want that.

#86 Find volunteers.

CLAUDIA & FRIENDS ...er instruction, because everyone has his/her own interpretation
IF YOU JUMP, I JUMP

Step 3: Try to capture the moment with your Polaroid camera.

Step 4: Watch and see how "jumping fever" takes over your immediate vicinity ... and always remember: If you jump, I jump.

Step 5: Tips: The photographer should kneel because then the jump looks higher. Outdoors is better than indoors (light, space). Summer is better than winter (less clothes, more mobility).

#87 Come up with the beginning of a story. Type it up

AVE (HEIDELBERGER, paste it on the letter and add a suitable photo. Number the photo on
AND FRIENDS the ... write the film type. Add
IMPOSSIBLE CHAIN LETTER

Step 2: Send everything to someone you like and kindly ask her/him to do the same. By a certain deadline, the last person to receive the chain letter should return everything to you.

Step 3: Involve the whole world.

Step 4: Be creative.

Step 5: Have fun.

#88 Select your favorite Impossible photos. Their size

WERONIKA GAJDA
COASTERS

Step 2: Use a laminating machine to protect them.
...minutes you will have your coasters ready.

Step 4: Now decide whom you want to invite for a drink or two.

#89 Take any photo you like.

ALAN MARCHESELLI ...listen to the picture.
IT'S MONDRIAN TIME

Step 3: Cut lines or forms you like.

Step 4: ...you are satisfied.

#90 Photograph your favorite building from all sides.

JOSIE KEEFE ...photos of each side, working from the ground up. Keep the number of photos...
HOUSE OF CARDS

Step 2: Once the photos have developed, tape each side together in order from the ground up. Cover the bottom white border with the top of the photo below, so that as much of the photograph as possible shows. Make sure each side is the same height.

Step 3: Build the building! Tape the backs of each side together.

Step 4: Stand back and enjoy!

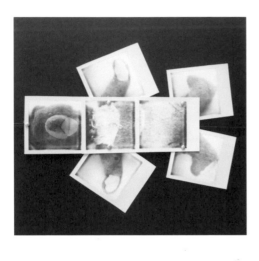

#93 Besides your favorite toy, you need scissors, a hole

BARBARA WERTH
JUMPING NICKY

Step 1: ...
one bead (or more), four coins and a close-up lens.

a favorite doll, teddy or any other soft toy you love from your childhood.

Step 3: Take photographs of all body parts: head, body, legs and arms.

Step 4: Put them together.

Step 5: Hang on the wall and enjoy!

#92 Make up a little story idea.

DANIEL DÖRING
IMPOSSIBLE FLIPBOOK

Step 2: ... illustrate it.
I recommend using a tripod to do so.
... to shoot and develop.

Step 4: Stack the photos.

Step 5: Secure the stack with a clip.

Step 6: Ta-da – your Impossible flipbook is ready!

#91 Set your goal and start training.

GUILLAUME POLLINO
HOW HIGH CAN YOU GO?

... your Polaroid camera and start climbing.
... go to shoot a possible photo?

Step 4: If you can go higher than 5,416m, please let us know.

Note: Please consult your doctor before accepting this challenge.

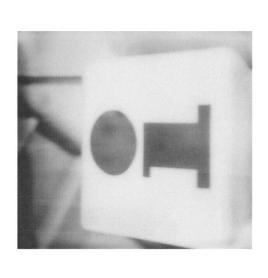

#96 *Step 1:* Walk through your city.

AVE HEIDELBERGER out for signs.

Step 3: Think of what you want to say and start writing!

CREATIVE WRITING

#95 *Step 1:* To thread sewing silk (or similar material)

LIA SÁANE the Impossible frame or directly through the picture, you will need to hammer holes into

STITCHES to put the needle through.

Step 2: After preparing the holes, you can make cross stitches, add embroidery or stitchery, or attach Impossibles to each other in a row, a mosaic, on top of each other or to anything else that can be attached to an Impossible photo in a similar way.

#94 *Step 1:* Select 24 of your favorite Impossible photos.

ULRIKE KÖBLER Number them from 1 – 24 on the back side.

IMPOSSIBLE ADVENT (with magnet sticks)

CALENDAR clock showing.

Step 4: Celebrate each day of Advent with an Impossible memory of the past year.

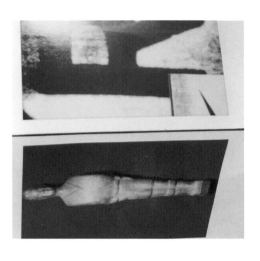

#99 Look for subjects that relate to the birthday child

RAUL DIAZ, and select items to serve as the letters

BIRTHDAY CARDS that you'll then use to form words.

Step 1: ... subjects, making sure they represent each letter needed for your birthday message.

Step 3: Shoot all photos and let them develop.

Step 4: Tape all photos together to create your message.

Step 5: Fold the photos accordion style. Now you have the most unique birthday card fold out ever.

#98 Mount the SX 70 on a tripod.

JIMMY LYAM

SX 70 LONG EXPOSURE

Step 1: ... picture through the viewfinder.

Step 3: Set the dial depending on the film you use.

Step 2: ... as long a ... exposure

Step 5: Shield the film from light and let it develop.

#97 Take photos of basic stuff you use in your

IMPOSSIBLE FACTORY TEAM

KITCHEN SUPPLY ... in three columns: in stock, to

CHAIN MANAGEMENT

Step 1: Create a chart according to your needs. We

Step 3: Arrange the photos of your supplies accordingly, to see what you still have or what you need to buy soon in order to keep your stomach filled.

#100 *Step 1* Gather your favorite colors, shapes and memories

ROSANNA DURSON / ANNA BARSON
DAISY CHAIN

Step 2: Select your favorite few and hole punch them at

Step 3: Thread onto the desired type of string and wear around your neck.

#101 *Step 1* Shoot a macro shot of your favorite body part.

FLORIAN KAPS
PICTURE IN PICTURE

Step 2: lens or, if not available, shoot from a billboard photo in device.

Step 3: Find a person who is Impossible enough to hold this photo in front of his/her own body.

Step 4: Attention: The better the dimensions match, the better the final result will be.

#102 *Step* our project isn't over!

YOU

Submit your works online and

Step 3: be part of the Impossible world.

Step 4: Register online at: www.the-impossible-project.com/10rways

ARE YOU FEELING INSPIRED TO PURSUE YOUR OWN IMPOSSIBLE WAY?

Discover the beauty and complexities of Impossible's new instant films for classic Polaroid cameras. These new materials behave differently than the old Polaroid films, but will develop nicely as long as you bear in mind a few important tips.

First of all, unlearn the way you shoot digital images in order to get confident again in shooting analog instant photos. This brief starter manual contains all you need to know to get ready to shoot:

Step 1: Find a classic Polaroid camera.

Step 2: Get the appropriate Impossible instant film.

Step 3: Familiarize yourself with the camera's settings, e.g. set the lighten/darken wheel to the correct setting, or adjust after your first shot for optimized results.

Step 4: Extreme cold or hot temperatures will affect your image results. The best is to shoot at temperatures of around 14–28°C/57–82°F

Step 5: Since the camera has no image stabilization, it's important to hold the camera steady, especially at low light levels, and to be patient while pressing the button until the photo is ejected.

Step 6: Shield the photo from light after it's ejected – the first seconds are crucial! Protect the photo from light for up to 3 minutes while it develops.

Step 7: The photo will take 5–30 minutes to develop completely, depending on the film type.

Step 8: Flip it over and enjoy your Impossible photo.

Step 9: Store Impossible color photos in a cool, dry place; dry Impossible black and white photos in the Impossible Dry Age Kit and store them upright.

Step 10: To be prepared for your next Impossible adventure, make sure to keep a stock of film ready. Refrigerate unopened film packs at 5–10°C/41–50°F, but do not freeze. Before shooting, allow the film to adjust to room temperature for at least 1 hour.

STILL HUNGRY? PLEASE VISIT WWW.THE-IMPOSSIBLE-PROJECT.COM/101WAYS FOR MORE IDEAS OR TO UPLOAD AND PRESENT AN IDEA OF YOUR OWN!

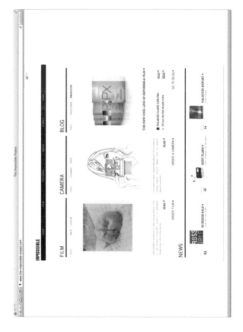

**PLEASE TURN THE PAGE
TO FIND ALL THE BASICS YOU'LL NEED
ON YOUR ANALOG JOURNEY.**

CLASSIC POLAROID CAMERAS

Over the course of its history Polaroid produced countless models of cameras for integral instant film. This overview is not complete, but presents a few of the most popular Polaroid camera types: SX 70, 600 and Image / Spectra. When you find one of these cameras in your grandparents' attic, in the closet at your father's studio, at a flea market in your home-town or somewhere in the world, you know that there will be film to load it with – Impossible instant films.

How to check whether a classic Polaroid camera is still able to shoot Impossible film:
Simply insert an empty film cassette and press the shutter. If you hear that famous sound and if it sounds like it's working well, you know the camera is ready to shoot. Before actually doing so, make sure the two metal rollers in the film compartment are clean. Any dirt or residue left on the rollers may cause an imprint on the photo.

600 ONE STEP RED STRIPE

SLR 680

SLR 680 LAND CAMERA

600 SUPERCOLOR 645 CL

IMAGE 1200FF

SX 70 LAND CAMERA

IMAGE PRO

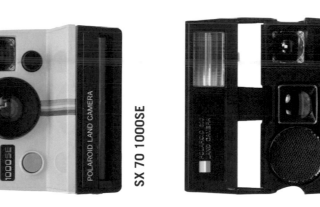

SX 70 SONAR ONE STEP

SUPERCOLOR 635CL

SPECTRA 2

SX 70 1000SE

660 SUN

IMAGE SYSTEM

SX 70 TIME-ZERO ONE STEP

600 TAZ LOONEY TUNES

ONE STEP CLOSE UP

WITH A LITTLE HELP FROM MY FRIENDS

Impossible is dedicated to promoting every type of analog experience you might possibly want to explore with instant photography. Some tools and materials to support your creative use of instant photos exist already, with more to come – inspired and suggested by Impossible users like you. Check out these smart and handy accessories that might be helpful to have at hand for your next analog instant project, along with your creativity and before rolling up your sleeves.

1

2

3

6

5

IM9OSSIBLE
MAGNETIC WALLSTARS

7

8

IM9OSSIBLE

LIFT IT

4

1 CREATIVE KIT Provides the basic equipment for emulsion lifts: water trays, a lift clip, a thermometer, a fountain pen filler, wooden clips and paper sheets. **2 LIFT IT! BRUSH SET** The set contains four brushes and a special soap exclusively manufactured for emulsion lifts with Impossible films. **3 LIFT IT! PAPER** Noble Vat and Smooth White are perfect carriers for emulsion lifts, guaranteeing good hold and fast drying. **4 COLD CLIP** Tells you whether the Impossible photo is too warm, too cold or just right. In addition, the pen included in the clip is ideal for image manipulation. **5 MAGNETIC WALLSTARS** Magnetic Wallstars attach Impossible photos to any metal surface, e.g. a fridge, desk lamp, computer or window frame. **6 INSTANT POSTCARDS** The set contains ten foldable postcards with self-adhesive insert for easily attaching Impossible PX format photos and mailing them to a good friend. **7 MAGNETIC FRAMES** These carefully hand-crafted frames feature a heavy premium metal frame and a clever magnetic system that makes filling and refilling very fast and very easy. **8 MAGNETIC LED FRAMES** With its soft lighting, the Magnetic LED Frame allows for a luminous presentation for transparencies. It is carefully handcrafted from selected, high-quality materials.

IMPOSSIBLE PROJECT SPACES AND FACTORY OUTLET

Members of the original Impossible factory team personally present a very special selection of unique films, directly from the machines and fresher than you will get them anywhere else. Only Fridays from 11:00 a.m. – 4:00 p.m

We'd love to see you at one of our Impossible Project Spaces around the world. These warm and energetic Impossible homes are full of everything we love, plus they put on inspiring workshops, exhibitions and events.

ENSCHEDE
Impossible Factory Outlet
Hoge Bothofstraat 45
7511ZA Enschede
The Netherlands

TOKYO
2F Oak Bld
1-20-5 Aobadai Meguro
Tokyo 153oo42 Japan

NEW YORK
425 Broadway, 5th Floor
New York, NY 10013

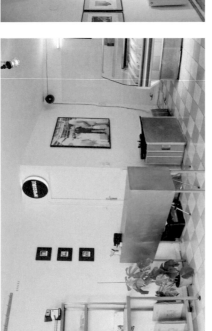

PARIS
77, rue Charlot
75003 Paris
France

VIENNA
Impossible Project Space Vienna
Kaiserstraße 74
1070 Vienna
Austria

IMPOSSIBLE PARTNER STORES

The people running our carefully selected Partner Stores are just as passionate about analog instant photography as we are. Dedicated to this medium, they offer the whole range of our products, including limited film editions, rare cameras and hand-selected accessories, as well as various events.

BARCELONA
Tantarantana 16
Born - Barcelona
Spain

BEIJING, UCCASTORE
798 Art District, No.4 Jiu Xian Qiao Lu
P.O. Box 8503, Chaoyang District
Beijing, China 100015

BERLIN, SOFORTBILD SHOP
Brunnenstr. 195
10119 Berlin
Germany

CLEVELAND, APERTURE
2541 Scranton Rd
Cleveland, OH 44113
USA

DECATUR, THE CAMERA DOCTOR
2090 North Decatur Road
Decatur, GA 30033
USA

DÜSSELDORF
Bilker Allee 180
40215 Düsseldorf
Germany

HONG KONG, MINT
2/F, 26A Russell Street
Causeway Bay
Hong Kong

KANAGAWA, SWEET ROAD
101 2-21 Minami saiwai cho saiwaiku kawaski
Kanagawa, 212-0016, Japan
+81 044-544-8177

KUALA LUMPUR, THE CLICK SHOP
Pavilion Kuala Lumpur
168, Jalan Bukit Bintang
55100, Kuala Lumpur, Malaysia

MANCHESTER, INCOGNITO
5 Stevenson Square
Manchester M1 1DN
United Kingdom

MILAN, CORNER STORE
Barbara Frigerio Contemporary Art
Via dell'Orso 12 entrata via Ciovasso
20121 Milano, Italy

MUNICH, FOTO AUGUSTIN
Nordendstr. 60
80801 Munich
Germany

OAK PARK, A&A STUDIOS
128 Harrison St.
Oak Park, IL 60304
USA

PHILADELPHIA, MIDTEK
3131 Walnut St.
Philadelphia, PA 19104
USA

ROME, CORNER STORE
Impossible Corner Store Rome
Via degli Scipioni 24
00192 Rome, Italy

INFORMATION

This book is published in conjunction with the creative challenge "101 Ways to Do Something Impossible" presented by The Impossible Project begun in fall 2011

EDITORS
The Impossible Project, Marlene Kelnreiter with a foreword by Dr. Florian Kaps

COPYEDITING
Ella Ornstein

TRANSLATIONS
Marlene Kelnreiter

CONCEPT AND GRAPHIC DESIGN
Heine/Lenz/Zizka, www.hlz.de
Nico Bats

TYPEFACE
Trade Gothic, Proforma

PAPER
Profigloss, Zeta Micro Natur

PRINTING
optimal media GmbH, Röbel

PUBLISHER
The Impossible Project
Halbgasse 3 / 2 / 1 1070 Vienna
Austria

Tel: +43 1 8903 190
Fax: +43 1 8903 190 15
www. the-impossible-project.com

ISBN 978-3-9503259-1-1
Printed in Germany, August 2012.

SAN FRANCISCO, PHOTOWORKS
2077-A Market St @ Church St
San Francisco, CA 94114
USA

SAN FRANCISCO, PHOTOBOOTH
1193 Valencia St @ 23rd
San Francisco, CA 94110
USA

SEATTLE, RARE MEDIUM
1321 E Pine St
Seattle, WA 98122
USA

SINGAPORE, PEEK!
36 Armenian Street
#01-04/02-04
Singapore 179934

SPARTANBURG, SPARTAN PHOTO CENTER
197 East Saint John Street
Spartanburg, SC 29302
USA

VANCOUVER, BEAU PHOTO
1520 West 6th Avenue
Vancouver, BC
Canada V6J 1R2

ZURICH, MUSEUM FÜR GESTALTUNG
Ausstellungsstrasse 60
CH-8005 Zürich
Switzerland

MORE IMPOSSIBLE DEALERS CAN BE FOUND NEARBY
As of today, in fall 2012, there are 137 dealers in more than 30 countries around the world who carry a selection of Impossible products, and every day we find more. To find your nearest Impossible dealer online, visit: www.the-impossible-project.com/stores

A Manual of
Construction
Documentation